Teacher as Counselor

Developing the Helping Skills You Need

D0067066

SURVIVAL SKILLS FOR TEACHERS SERIES

Teacher as Counselor
Developing the Helping Skills You Need
Jeffrey A. Kottler and Ellen Kottler

Crack-Affected Children
A Teacher's Guide
Mary Bellis Waller

Teacher as Counselor

Developing the Helping Skills You Need

Jeffrey A. Kottler
Ellen Kottler

CORWIN PRESS, INC.
A Sage Publications Company
Newbury Park, California

Copyright © 1993 by Corwin Press, Inc.

For information address:

Corwin Press, Inc.
A Sage Publications Company
2455 Teller Road
Newbury Park, California 91320

SAGE Publications Ltd.
6 Bonhill Street
London EC2A 4PU
United Kingdom

SAGE Publications India Pvt. Ltd.
M-32 Market
Greater Kailash I
New Delhi 110 048 India

Printed in the United States of America

Library of Congress Cataloging-in-Publication Data

Kottler, Jeffrey A.
  Teacher as counselor : developing the helping skills you need /
Jeffrey A. Kottler, Ellen Kottler.
      p.   cm.—(Survival skills for teachers)
  Includes bibliographical references.
  ISBN 0-8039-6050-6
  1. Teacher participation in educational counseling—United States.
2. Teacher-student relationships—United States. I. Kottler,
Ellen. II. Title. III. Series.
LB1027.5.K666 1993
371.4'046'0973—dc20   92-42781

93 94 95 96   10 9 8 7 6 5 4 3 2 1

Corwin Press Production Editor: Marie Louise Penchoen

Contents

Preface

Modern day teachers, by necessity, do so much more than present content and information to children. In fact, actual time spent lecturing in the classroom represents less than half of the teacher's daily responsibilities. This reality is especially ironic considering the amount of time teacher education programs spend on helping educators become experts in their content areas and proficient in the materials, methods, and management of pedagogical presentations.

In addition to their teaching duties and responsibilities as classroom managers, teachers are called on to do a variety of things for which they may feel unprepared:

1. Respond to children's emotional needs
2. Resolve interpersonal conflicts
3. Conduct parent conferences
4. Identify children suffering from abuse, neglect, drug abuse, and a variety of emotional problems, and make appropriate referrals when necessary
5. Assess children's developmental transitions and guide their continued physical, emotional, social, and spiritual growth, in addition to their cognitive development

6. Participate in Individualized Education Programs (IEPs)
7. Function as a problem solver for those children in the throes of crisis.

In short, even though they have had precious little training in these specialties, teachers function as counselors and consultants.

The intent of this book is not to equip beginning teachers with the background or the skills to function in the role of counselor or human relations consultant—that is what school counselors, psychologists, and social workers do. The reality of daily school life, however, is that teachers must often serve in helping roles beyond their responsibilities as content experts. As they stand before their classes lecturing about history, they cannot help but notice the children who seem tired or sad or troubled. As they sit at their desks grading papers, they will be visited by children who trust them, children who want someone to listen to them and understand them. As they speak with parents or other colleagues about children in their charge, they will be required to demonstrate a high degree of interpersonal sensitivity and skill. It is our hope, therefore, that this small book will introduce beginning teachers to the basic methodology of counseling and consulting. Although we cannot make a counselor out of a teacher in a format as limited as this (years of supervised practice are needed), we certainly can sensitize educators to the basic ideas and skills that are involved in being a helper.

The Audience

Teacher as Counselor is intended for two audiences quite similar to one another. It can be used as a primary or secondary text in a variety of education courses that include a component on "helping skills" for teachers. Indeed, many teacher preparation programs include a whole class on the role of educator as counselor/consultant. In other countries training models exist in which counseling as a specialty in education is unheard of; teachers are expected to function as counselors in addition to their other responsibilities. Who, after all, spends more time with children and is better positioned to observe them on a daily basis?

The second audience is the population of beginning teachers who are just launching their careers. Many school districts see the need to augment traditional teacher preparation programs with additional training in areas that are often neglected in universities. Among the highest priorities is to ensure that newly hired personnel are equipped with professional and personal "survival" skills that are likely to increase the new teacher's probability of success. Counseling and consulting skills certainly rate high on the list of beginning teachers who are trying so hard to earn the trust and respect of their children.

A Note to Readers

The subjects discussed in this book do not lend themselves to learning by passive means. Although reading chapters about helping skills will enable you to conceptualize how and why various counseling strategies are applied, there is no way these complex behaviors can become part of your own interpersonal style without considerable practice. This personal integration can take two basic forms:

1. After each idea is presented, ask yourself how you can make it part of your life, how you could use the techniques to enrich your relationships.
2. Find opportunities to practice new skills in enough situations so that they will become a natural part of your interpersonal style.

At the end of each chapter we have included a list of suggested readings should you want to learn more about a particular subject. Of even more importance, we have provided a number of activities that you might complete if you want to apply what you learn to real-life situations. This kind of practice is, of course, one of the most important concepts of effective education: If we expect to influence the way students think, feel, and act, we must develop structures in which they can apply what they learn in multiple situations. It certainly applies to your own attempts to master a set of very difficult skills in a very short period of time.

With sufficient time and energy and commitment on your part, with a systematic study of helping skills, and with supervised practice in applying them, you *can* become proficient at integrating counseling and consulting interventions as part of your daily teaching roles.

We gratefully acknowledge the assistance of Gracia Alkema, Elaine Jarchow, Rebecca Mills, and Betsy Morgan in the preparation of this manuscript.

JEFFREY A. KOTTLER
ELLEN KOTTLER

About the Authors

Jeffrey A. Kottler is an associate professor of counseling and educational psychology at the University of Nevada, Las Vegas. He has studied at Oakland University, Harvard University, Wayne State University, and the University of Stockholm and received his Ph.D. degree from the University of Virginia. He has worked as a counselor in a variety of settings including hospitals, mental health centers, schools, clinics, universities, corporations, and private practice.

Kottler is the author or co-author of twelve books including *Private Moments, Secret Selves: Enriching Our Time Alone* (1990), *The Compleat Therapist* (1991), *Introduction to Therapeutic Counseling* (2nd edition, 1992), *Compassionate Therapy: Working With Difficult Clients* (1992), *On Being a Teacher* (1993), and *Group Leadership for Advanced Practitioners* (1993).

Ellen Kottler received her B.A. degree from the University of Michigan, her M.A. degree from Eastern Michigan University, and is working toward her Ed.D. degree at the University of Nevada, Las Vegas. She has been a teacher for over twenty years in public and private schools, universities, alternative schools, and adult education programs. She has worked in inner city schools, as well as suburban and rural settings and has taught history, mathematics, Spanish, social studies, humanities, and family living.

To

Charles and Fay Isackson

The Multiple Hats
of Classroom Teachers

Quick! What comes to mind when you think about being a teacher? You probably imagine standing in front of a room of eager students who hang on your every word as you deliver a sizzling and exciting presentation that utterly captivates their interest. For generations of educators since the days of Socrates, members of our profession have been judged primarily on their skill as orators and lecturers. Indeed, presenting content, leading discussions, and showing videos are the lifeblood of the teacher's role. By no means, however, are these the *only* things that teachers do, nor is "disseminator of information" the most important role that you will play.

When you reminisce about your own educational experiences and reflect on those teachers who were most inspirational, who made the greatest difference in your life, we suspect that you recall things more intangible than their well-honed teaching skills. There was something about their personal qualities, the ways they carried themselves, their integrity and honesty, that earned your respect and trust. It was not just the knowledge they held that made them such wonderful teachers—

it was the personal and passionate way in which they communicated their caring for you.

Assuming this phenomenon is fairly universal—in other words,
that students are influenced not only by instruction but by a
teacher's caring and compassion—then teachers really must
have specialized training in all their various roles. You have had
systematic education in the materials and methods of peda-
gogy, in constructing lesson plans and completing individual
progress reports, and in using audio-visual and computer tech-
nology. But what about training in the other roles you will play
in students' lives—as a model of personal effectiveness, as a
compassionate listener, as a skilled helper?

You will be called on daily, if not hourly, to wear a number of
different hats and to function in a variety of diverse roles for
which you may not be adequately prepared. What will you do
when a child confides to you that she is pregnant? How will
you handle the student who is emotionally falling apart before
your eyes? What will you do when you suspect that a child is
abusing drugs or is suffering from an eating disorder? What
will you say to the child who approaches you for understanding
because he feels lonely? What will you do when a student
solicits your promise to keep a secret, but then tells you that she
is breaking the law and intends to continue doing so?

Teachers are not just receptacles of knowledge who impart
pearls of wisdom every time a bell rings. By choosing this
profession, you have dedicated yourself to influencing children's
lives. To accomplish this mission you will do so much more
than stand before a classroom of attentive eyes and ears. You
will develop relationships with children that are built on trust,
mutual respect, and true affection. And from those alliances,
children will come to you with their problems. But more often,
they will cry out for help in more subtle ways via signs that you
will not be able to read without additional training.

Your job is to develop yourself as a skilled helper, a task that
will involve mastering a number of counseling and consulting
skills. This training will permit you to observe and make sense
of what children are thinking, feeling, and doing. It will allow
you to gain access into their inner worlds, to earn their trust,

and to truly understand what they are experiencing. From such an empathic position you will help them feel understood. You will help them reach greater clarity. You will help them make difficult decisions. When indicated, you will urge them to seek professional help. And they will listen to you because you have the helping skills and an authentic interest in their welfare.

Counseling Skills for Teachers

Teachers in other countries function quite differently than we do in North America. In Singapore, for example, there are no school counselors—not because of lack of funds but rather because of recognition that teachers are the ones who are best positioned to serve in counseling roles. They are the ones, after all, who interact with children on a daily basis. If a child is going to approach an adult for assistance or advice, it will probably not be the person who arranges her schedule once per semester; it will be with the teacher who she has come to trust over many hours of work and play together.

Whether you like it or not, whether you prepare for the role or not, you will be sought out as a confidante of children who have nowhere else to turn. They will expect a number of things from you, some that you cannot deliver (finding the "right" answer), and some that you should not do (take over their lives and tell them what to do). Nevertheless, if you are equipped with some counseling skills, just some basic helping strategies like listening and responding, you will be amazed at the services you can render in helping children gain better clarity of their feelings, better understanding of their motives, and greater resolve in following through on a plan to change their behavior. Adding counseling skills to your repertoire of educational methodologies will help you in a number of ways:

1. You will notice an improvement in your personal relationships. Because learning counseling skills will increase your sensitivity and responsiveness, this training will affect the ways you relate to other people. You will notice yourself become more attuned

to others' feelings. You will become more clear in your communications, more expressive of your own needs. Finally, you will
experience a renewed commitment to work toward greater
intimacy in your relationships with friends and family.

2. You will become more respected as a colleague in your school. Just
as high-level interpersonal skills allow you to create better
relationships in your personal life, they give you the confidence
and ability to forge constructive alliances with administrators,
other teachers in your school, and support staff. Everyone
wants a friend who listens well, who is empathic, who is a clear
thinker, and who responds to one's needs. One other benefit:
When you learn to speak the language of counselors, you will
be able to make more appropriate referrals of children in need
of help.

3. You will become more influential in your work in the classroom.
Children respond best to teachers who model what they themselves would some day like to become. They respect you and
respond to you not only for your expertise but also for your
caring and compassion. Counseling skills will, quite simply,
allow you to create better relationships with children in a shorter
period of time. Students will be more inclined to trust you and
to work hard to gain your respect if they sense the same from
you. These skills thus form the glue bonding together everything else you have learned about being a superlative teacher.

*4. You will be able to address children's most important concerns at
the same time you counteract your own fears of ineptitude and failure.*
Beginning teachers, in particular, have a myriad of apprehensions
regarding their own abilities and potential as professionals.
Several teacher education students, on the verge of beginning
their student teaching, talk about some of their greatest fears.

Karyn feels quite confident about her ability to relate to children; however, she feels most unprepared conducting parent conferences: "I dread having to explain to parents why I do things the
way I do. I don't know how on earth I will ever get them to try
different things at home that will make my job easier."

Randi, as well, worries most about how she will react to certain parents—especially the ones who don't seem to care about their children: "I'm afraid I will lose my temper, become completely out of control, when I talk to some of these parents who do such damage to their kids. I know if I do that I will just end up hurting the kids as well as my own situation."

Travis mentions his greatest fear as encountering the child who is being neglected or abused at home: "I know what I am *supposed* to do: report the situation to protective services. But sometimes things aren't so clear. What happens to the child after I do that? Maybe I'll just make things worse. I just hope I have the courage to do what is right."

Tanya is quite nervous about her responsibility being a model for kids: "It is so scary to think that everything I do and say will be watched so closely. Children are so impressionable, and I certainly would like to be the kind of person whom they admire. That is going to be hard for me because I'm not used to that kind of responsibility. I was the youngest in my family and used to looking up to everyone else."

Nick wonders if he will ever learn to disconnect from the intense emotional problems that he will encounter as a special education teacher: "Will I be able to save enough of myself for my family when I get home? Some of these kids are just so messed up and so needy—they just need so much attention. If I am going to last very long, I know I will have to back off, to separate their problems from my own."

Cassie is reluctantly honest in admitting she has a problem with patience: "It boggles my mind to think that I will be in a room with 30 kindergartners for 6 hours every day. Will I have the restraint to be gentle when some of the little ones try to push me over the edge?" She also wonders if she will be able to keep her biases under wraps: "I know we are all prejudiced to some extent. I just hope that I can withhold my judgments when I am dealing with a troubled student. Such a volatile situation could have disastrous results if I am not able to keep my own opinions to myself."

Nila considers herself oversensitive to criticism and overly cautious about everything she says. She wonders how that will affect her ability to be helpful: "I become obsessed with saying the 'right' thing the 'right' way. I don't want to hurt or embarrass anyone. I'm concerned that I won't do anything at all because I don't want to make any mistakes."

Each of these examples illustrates another way that counseling skills will help you neutralize your own fears of failure in trying to be helpful to children. That is the wonder and power of this training: As you become more skilled and accomplished as a helper of others, you become more proficient at applying what you know to your own life.

Life Inside the Classroom

Teaching is, first and foremost, a helping profession. While structuring a learning environment, the educator has to be aware of students' physical, emotional, and social needs, as well as their intellectual needs. Teachers must create a pleasant atmosphere in their classrooms where students will be safe physically and secure psychologically to explore the world of ideas. From the moment the students enter the room the teacher begins to develop a rapport with them and build trust—whether they stay for forty-five minutes or the whole day. The educator must be kind and helpful, inviting and stimulating, as students are guided through learning activities. The teacher must work toward building the self-respect and self-esteem of each student. Furthermore, he or she must work toward fostering tolerance and cooperation in the classroom. The teacher must prepare the children to interact with one another in a positive, constructive manner. Students must learn to be good citizens, to interpret the events taking place around them, and how to make decisions. It is the teacher's responsibility to provide these experiences.

In addition to these roles, the educator must get to know each student, his or her ups and downs, the momentary and long-term stresses of each individual. The teacher must offer support and encouragement to each child—to Hugo who lost a portion of his finger in an accident, to Amy whose new baby brother came home the night before, to Brian whose father moved out of the house last week. Changing friendships, fear of failure, and other issues occupy the minds of students. And the teacher must decide how best to approach the events that take place in the lives of children—one-to-one, through reading a story, or group discussion.

At the same time, the teacher must pay attention to external events that disrupt the daily schedule. Change interrupts the learning process whether it is an impromptu pep assembly, fire drill, or academic testing. A crisis in the community will take precedence over any planned topic. In several cities, for example, riots have distracted kids from concentrating on relatively less important priorities such as homework. Children needed to be reassured that they were safe and nothing would harm them. They talked about the impact of violence; for example, in one city, how far they had to go to get food stamps after the welfare office had been burned. Immediate needs had to be addressed. Similarly, students in another town talked about depression, loneliness, and the responsibilities of friendship after one student tried to commit suicide.

Life Outside the Classroom

A teacher will interact with counselors, social workers, school psychologists, deans, principals, parents, and other teachers on a regular basis. Whether evaluating the present or planning for the future, discussing a new policy or the behavior of an individual student, the teacher will be called on to give his or her views and recommendations. To work cooperatively with other professionals and parents, the teacher must also be able to establish rapport with these adults.

Relationships with students and other professionals are always evolving. Our goal is to provide the reader with the inspiration and motivation to develop the interpersonal skills so vital for the effective teacher. Perhaps you will develop a clearer idea of what will be expected of you if you watch over the shoulder of one professional who goes about fulfilling her daily roles as a teacher.

A Day in the Life

As Mrs. Neubrith opens the door to her car and prepares to gather her things together to start her day, she sees a group of teenagers congregating together by the side of the building. Her heart skips a beat: Will she have to break up a fight? Or perhaps they are transacting some illicit business that she will have to stop? No, this time she discovers an innocent gathering of friends who are huddled together for protection against the cold. She breathes a sigh of relief.

It is 7:10 in the morning and already Mrs. Neubrith, high school teacher extraordinaire, is beginning the first of several hundred interactions she will have throughout the day with different children and colleagues. As she approaches the door and mentally reviews what lies ahead, besides her usual teaching responsibilities, she knows that she will talk to one of the assistant principals about a new student in her class. She needs to get in to see the principal about a workshop she would like to attend that will require supplemental funding. One of her lunch partners is going through a divorce, so she knows that will be a focus of discussion during the day. Also, she had been alerted that someone from the district office would be monitoring some of her classes for a research study he is conducting. She wonders if that is his real intent or perhaps it is another in a series of evaluations.

During her preparation period Mrs. Neubrith will talk to the school counselor about one of her students who is tracked in college prep but has much more interest in going into the military. As the day continues, a student who flunked her driver's test will literally cry on her shoulder. She will catch a student cheating in her fourth hour class, a situation that will involve speaking to the other assistant principal, the student twice, and the student's parents who will adamantly refuse to acknowledge that their darling son could have committed such an immoral act. Another student will approach her with excitement at having recently become engaged; this student feels a special affinity for Mrs. Neubrith because she and her fiance first met in her class.

An assortment of other interactions will take place with the school secretary, several colleagues who are organizing support groups for children of divorce, and literally hundreds of children who pass her in the halls. Mrs. Neubrith tries to acknowledge each person and realizes they want so much more from her than she can possibly deliver. "I am so grateful," Mrs. Neubrith reminds herself for the umpteenth time, "that I invested the time to learn some basic counseling and communication skills to supplement what I do in the classroom."

As you follow Mrs. Neubrith through an all-too-typical day, you notice the great number of people she comes into contact with and the variety of situations in which she uses her interpersonal skills. One moment she is talking to a student who is apprehensive about a family move; she moves on to talk to a boy who feels like a failure because he was cut from the baseball team; then, she speaks to a student who is returning from drug rehabilitation; next, she is advising a student about college plans. A great portion of her day is spent interacting with others as people turn to her for guidance and as she lets others know she cares about what is happening to them.

Whether you like it or not, whether you are prepared or not, students seek out teachers for help in making decisions about everything from accepting a party invitation to what classes they should take. They ask for help in sorting out values and evaluating the ethics of the situations they face. They come to share the events that take place in their lives: a new dog, frustration over a bad grade, rejected friendship, a death in the family. They turn to teachers with questions of manners and etiquette.

The ways you respond to these situations, the fluency and ease with which you switch the multiple hats you wear, will influence greatly the quality of the educational experiences you provide. Your knowledge of counseling skills will affect your relationships with the children you work with, your friendships and affiliations with colleagues, and even the quality of intimacy with the people you love the most.

Suggested Activities

1. What aspects of teaching are you most apprehensive about? What roles do you feel most unprepared for? After reflecting on these questions, (a) write down your responses and put the pages in a safe place where you can reread what you wrote several years from now, and (b) share your reactions in a group of peers meeting to discuss their fears.
2. Interview a cross section of children representing different grade levels to find out the roles they would like to see teachers play in their lives. Encourage them to be as specific as possible in describing what teachers could do to be helpful to them.
3. Shadow a teacher for a day and note the variety of roles that he or she plays with an assortment of different people. Organize your observations of the teacher's behavior into some broad categories of roles that were played—as lecturer, problem solver, secretary, or whatever.

Suggested Readings

Heck, S. F., & Williams, C. R. (1984). *The complex roles of the teacher: An ecological perspective.* New York: Teachers College Press.

Pullias, E. V., & Young, J. D. (1968). *A teacher is many things.* Bloomington: Indiana University Press.

Ram Das, & Gorman, P. (1985). *How can I help? Stories and reflections on service.* New York: Knopf.

Zehm, S., & Kottler, J. (1993). *On being a teacher: The human dimension.* Newbury Park, CA: Corwin.

Assessing Children's Problems

Assessment is an important part of a teacher's job. You have been taught to recognize a number of children's difficulties, including academic underachievement, cognitive deficits, learning disabilities, behavioral problems, and signs of child abuse. Yet these areas of difficulty represent, proportionately, only a small segment of what children struggle with in their daily lives. They are fighting to establish themselves as autonomous, confident, and competent human beings. They are working through a number of developmental transitions related to achieving physical, cognitive, emotional, and moral maturity. They are recovering from the stresses and strains of family and peer pressure, trying desperately to find a place in the world where they belong. They are trying to make a number of important life decisions about school, friends, work, and the future. And these are only the predictable and normal problems of adjustment that children encounter.

About one in five students in your classes is suffering from emotional difficulties not considered part of normal childhood adjustment. These children are highly anxious, so much so that they develop psychosomatic illnesses and stress-related symptoms such as chronic headaches, stomachaches, ulcers, and insomnia. Depression is also quite common among school-age children, a condition that often goes overlooked because these kids tend to be withdrawn, passive, and listless—not the sort to draw attention to themselves. Some of these kids are potentially suicidal and spend an inordinate amount of time planning their own demise, all while staring blankly at the blackboard. Still other children are hiding symptoms of drug abuse or eating disorders.

You will, of course, already have noticed those who have the more dramatic signs of severe personality disorders, but the vast majority of children's problems are overlooked by teachers who are not trained to notice their warning signs.

The Assessment Process

The most critical component of any treatment plan designed to help children in need is to assess accurately the nature of their difficulties. Assume, for instance, a child sits quietly in class, rarely contributing to discussions. His eyes are downcast, his posture slumped. He almost never interacts with other children, nor has he ever engaged you in any conversation. Does this child have an emotional problem, and if so, what is its nature?

That is a very good question indeed, one without a definitive answer. This child's behavior could mean any number of things— that he is chronically shy, that he is depressed, that he feels alienated and lonely, that he suffers from an autistic or schizoid disorder in which he is disconnected from the human race, that he is on drugs or overmedicated, that he has been kept up at night and is tired, perhaps even that he is a member of a culture in which his behavior is considered socially appropriate. Each of these possible diagnoses would suggest a different method of intervention and a different professional who you might consult for help.

It is not enough to sense that something is wrong with a child; you must also have a rough idea of what is going on before you can take appropriate action, whether that is to contact parents, social welfare, the school counselor, a physician, or whomever.

This process of systematically observing behavior, determining if it indicates some underlying difficulty, narrowing down the possibilities to a few reasonable hypotheses, and then initiating some form of action, resembles the differential diagnostic methods of physicians and psychologists. Your job is to figure out if indeed there is a serious problem, and if so, what to do about it.

Essentially you will be asking yourself a series of questions:

- What is unusual about this child's behavior?
- Is there a pattern to what I have observed?
- What information do I need to make an informed judgment?
- Who might I contact to collect this background?
- What are the risks of waiting longer to figure out what is going on?
- Does this child seem to be in any imminent danger?
- What can I do to build a better relationship with the child?
- Who can I consult about this case?

It is certainly beyond the scope of your role as a teacher to be able to diagnose accurately a host of emotional disorders, to be able to differentiate them from one another, and then to prescribe corresponding treatments. However, it is perfectly reasonable that with added training and supervised experience, you would become proficient in recognizing some of the signs of a child who is in trouble. We will review some of the more common disorders and difficulties you will encounter, list the most prevalent symptoms you might observe, and then mention the usual treatment strategies so that you can take appropriate action or make informed referrals.

Generalized Anxiety

Description: Excessive worry and apprehension over things that are out of one's control or in which the reaction is exaggerated beyond what is reasonable.

Example: A child agonizes continuously over school, sports, and social performance. He expresses persistent concern over possible harm that may befall his parents and so is reluctant to separate from them.

Symptoms: Nausea, stomachaches, headaches, sweating, dry mouth, frequent urination, dizziness, agitation, restlessness, irritability.

Usual interventions: Give lots of reassurance, use relaxation training and stress management, provide an opportunity to talk about fears and learn alternative ways to handle them, refer for counseling, make a referral to rule out associated physical maladies.

Phobic Disorders

Description: Avoidant and anxious responses to specific situations, such as being in open spaces (agoraphobia), separating from a parent (separation anxiety), social situations (social phobia), or spiders, snakes, high places, and so on (simple phobia).

Example: A child develops a persistent refusal to go to school after an embarrassing experience. She refuses to leave her parent's side when she is forcibly dragged away from home.

Symptoms: Persistent fears, physical sensations (sweating, heart palpitations, trembling, nausea, numbness, dizziness), avoidance of threatening stimulus.

Usual interventions: Teachers will want to work very closely with a therapist who can design a treatment program containing cognitive and behavioral components. Family counseling may be indicated. In school phobia cases, gradual desensitization is introduced. Teachers can be helpful by creating a supportive atmosphere.

Depression

Description: A pervasive mood disorder in which the child feels sad and withdrawn, with muted affect. There are several different kinds of depression: *endogenous depression* is a biologically based disorder that is caused by a neurochemical imbalance in the body; *dysthymia* is another chronic but less serious mood disorder in which there is no serious disruption of sleep, appetite, or daily functioning; *reactive depression* is an acute response to some crisis or distressing situation (grief, adjustment to life changes, and so on).

Example: A child has recently moved to the district from another city. He appears very quiet, reticent, and withdrawn. Sometimes you can see tears welling up in his eyes. He keeps to himself mostly and does not initiate interaction with other children.

Symptoms: In mild cases: sadness following an identifiable stressful event that precipitated the symptoms, low energy, poor concentration, low self-esteem, no history of recurrent episodes. In severe cases: disruption of normal functioning, appetite loss, sleep disruption, weight loss or gain, listlessness, abject hopelessness, rumination, suicidal thoughts and possible intent.

Usual interventions: Mild, reactive depression responds quite well to supportive relationships in which the child has the opportunity to express feelings and learn alternative ways of thinking about his or her predicament. Time is usually the best healer.

Severe endogenous depression, on the other hand, is potentially life threatening without intervention. In some cases intensive psychotherapy in addition to medication is required. The teacher can play a crucial role by making sure the child does receive expert help.

Suicide Potential

Although it is relatively common for children (and adults) to contemplate suicide during times of stress, here are some specific warning signs to watch for that indicate the potential for serious intent:

1. Toward the end of the school year when risks increase
2. Use of drugs or alcohol
3. Extensive preoccupation with death fantasies

4. Absence of a support system
5. The child has a specific plan as to how he or she would do it
6. The child has the means available to carry out the plan (a loaded gun or bottle of sleeping pills in the home)
7. A history of self-destructive acts
8. A gesture on the part of the child that may be interpreted as a cry for help
9. A history of a relative having killed him- or herself (providing a model of an acceptable way out)
10. Significant mood changes from depression to elation
11. Noticeable changes in a child's appearance or academic performance

Also important to keep in mind: Urban children are at greater risk than rural children, and certain minority groups (Native Americans) have higher-than-average suicide rates.

Prevention is critically important. Teachers can be most helpful by creating an atmosphere in their classes in which everyone is responsible for everyone else's welfare. Almost 90% of children who attempt suicide tell somebody of their intent—a friend, a parent, a teacher. By alerting children to the risk we can recruit their assistance in preventing tragedy. Keep in mind, however, that predicting suicidal acts is not an exact science; it is better to be cautious and conservative when you suspect a child is at risk and consult a counselor.

Attention Deficit Hyperactivity Disorders

Description: High degrees of impulsivity, unrestrained energy, and inattention that are not typical for the age of the child. The behavior is manifested in a number of settings, in school as well as home, and seriously impairs the child's ability to concentrate or perform assigned tasks.

Example: A child is performing poorly in school in spite of an apparent high degree of intelligence. She almost always appears restless, practically vibrating with energy as her attention wanders from one thing to another without pause. The more concentration that is required for a particular task in school, the more frustrated she becomes.

Symptoms: Restless or fidgeting behavior, difficulty staying in one place for a period of time, easily distracted, impulsive behavior in class, wandering attention from assigned tasks that are rarely completed, talks excessively or constantly interrupts others, has difficulty listening to and following instructions.

Usual interventions: Structured individual assignments that are within the child's threshold of attentiveness; tight external boundaries; medication for severe cases.

Conduct Disorder

Description: A persistent pattern of abusing the rights of others with little regard for established rules. This child will appear unduly aggressive, even cruel in his or her destructive, violent, or antisocial behavior.

Example: A child explodes with temper tantrums when he does not get his way. He is provocative and seems oblivious to other children's feelings. He is often discovered to be starting fights, stealing others' things, doing anything to get his way. Furthermore, he shows no guilt or remorse over his actions. He feels entitled to get his way whenever he wants and views others as his personal slaves.

Symptoms: A pattern of cruelty toward animals or other age mates; participation in frequent fights; deliberate destruction of others' property; either alone or as a leader of others, he initiates aggressive acts.

Usual interventions: Set very strict boundaries with immediate enforcement of consequences for noncompliance with rules; improve frustration tolerance through gradual presentation of more challenging tasks; family counseling to work on consistent parenting; inpatient treatment for severe cases.

Oppositional Disorder

Description: A less severe version of a conduct disorder in which the child shows a pattern of being hostile, defiant, and uncooperative. This behavior is not necessarily universal but may appear only in certain settings (at home, in certain classes, when around certain people, in response to certain stimuli). This child does show some concern for others' rights and does not deliberately hurt others in attempts to protect herself.

Example: A child appears surly, hostile, even ferocious in her opposition to you and things you ask of her. When you ask her to do something, she outright refuses, or sometimes even does the exact opposite. You can hear her swear at you behind your back and feel her disdain for you and everything you stand for.

Symptoms: Frequent loss of temper; situational arguments with authority figures; a pattern of defiance, vindictiveness, and annoying others; common swearing and dramatic rebellion.

Usual interventions: Set limits and enforce them without retribution; examine your own contributions to precipitating the oppositional behavior; schedule individual conferences to confront the behavior nondefensively and work on a more empathic alliance. Unlike children suffering from conduct disorders, these children respond quite well to a teacher's systematic attempts to improve self-esteem, frustration tolerance, emotional control, and aggression. They also respond well to counseling because they must develop cooperative relationships with an authority figure during the process.

Eating Disorders

Description: A disturbance in eating behavior characterized by significant weight loss and obsession with food (anorexia nervosa), episodes of binging and forced vomiting (bulimia), or persistent eating of non-nutritious substances such as paint, chalk, plaster, paper, leaves, and so on (pica).

Example: You have noticed that one of the girls in your class is as "skinny as a rail," yet you have occasionally overheard her remark to friends how fat she is. She has low self-esteem. You recall that she was once much heavier and began to lose weight after her relationship with a boyfriend ended.

Symptoms: The prevalence of anorexia nervosa and bulimia occur almost exclusively among girls, especially in adolescence; perfectionistic behavior; mild obesity before onset of weight loss; excessive concern for food but poor eating habits; distorted body image.

Usual interventions: Because in virtually all cases the child's friends and family know about her unusual eating habits, teachers can do a lot to educate children on the signs of trouble and the dangerous consequences of these disorders. In severe cases, eating disorders are potentially lethal without hospitalization. In more moderate cases, family counseling and behavior modification are often successful.

Schizophrenia

Description: A distinct distortion of reality in the presence of hallucinations, delusions, or bizarre behavior. Although other diagnoses are possible (schizoaffective disorder, brief psychotic reaction) depending on duration of symptoms and subtle variations, you will notice fairly marked deviations from normal functioning.

Example: An adolescent girl has been acting progressively more bizarre in school. Other children shy away from her and make fun of her; she seems oblivious to their teasing, to anything really. She speaks in nonsensical phrases, stares blankly out the window, and claims that she sometimes hears voices.

Symptoms: Presence of unusual behavior for a least one week; the presence of delusions or hallucinations; incoherent and disconnected speech; inappropriate emotional reactions; strange, delusional beliefs; social withdrawal; peculiar behavior.

Usual interventions: The prognosis is most favorable the sooner intervention takes place; conversely, the longer the symptoms go on the more likely the child will not fully recover. The treatment usually consists of brief hospitalization, medication to control delusional thinking, and psychotherapy to help the child readjust. Because early detection is so crucial to recovery, teachers can be instrumental in helping the child by referring him or her for professional help.

Substance Abuse Disorders

Description: The addiction to, dependence on, or habitual use of alcohol, marijuana, cocaine, barbiturates, amphetamines, or other substances to the extent that normal functioning is impaired.

Example: A child in your class repeatedly falls asleep and appears lethargic when he is awake. His eyes sometimes appear glassy, his speech slurred. There has been a noticeable change in his behavior and academic performance over the course of several weeks. You happen to know that the friends that he has been hanging around with are regular users of drugs and alcohol.

Symptoms: Frequent use of a psychoactive substance in increasing amounts; little control over the amount and frequency of substance that is ingested; a lot of time spent thinking about the drug; social and school activities disrupted; impairment in functioning that may be manifested in slurred speech, shaky gait, glassy or bloodshot eyes, irritability, hyperactivity, or lethargy.

Usual interventions: A supportive relationship with a teacher can be a catalyst for a student to break away from self-destructive habits. The treatment of these problems is very difficult because they involve both a physical habit or addiction and social reinforcement among one's peer group. Referral to a specialist in substance abuse disorders is usually indicated because the child may need fairly drastic disruption of his or her usual life routines in order to recover fully. Brief hospitalization is often suggested along with family counseling, individual counseling, and re-education. By far, prevention is the best treatment, and teachers play a major role in addressing the risks before behavior gets out of hand.

Obsessive Compulsive Disorder

Description: Recurrent thoughts (obsessions) or repetitive behaviors (compulsions) beyond one's control. They are usually senseless ideas or actions that represent attempts to ward off other concerns through ritualistic action.

Example: A child meticulously arranges every aspect of her desk before she will attempt any project. She is insistent that everything be absolutely in its correct place and refuses to do any work unless everything is in order. She rarely completes any of her work because of her inordinate concern for arranging materials.

Symptoms: Repetitive behavior or recurrent thoughts that keep anxiety under control; images or impulses are intrusive and render the person at least minimally dysfunctional.

Usual interventions: The earlier the obsessive thinking or compulsive behavior is detected, the greater the likelihood that it can be treated; behavior therapy is the preferred intervention; medication is also sometimes effective.

Somatization Disorder

Description: A long-standing series of physical complaints without any apparent organic cause. This disorder represents the body's attempt to metabolize stress. The child is distressed by the symptoms and is not faking them.

Example: A child constantly complains of stomach aches. He has been taken to a number of specialists but they have found no cause for the trouble.

Symptoms: Preoccupation with some problem in the body for which there is no known physical cause. Common symptoms include abdominal pain, back pain, or headaches.

Usual interventions: Rule out completely the possibility of any medical condition; focus on improving functioning in school and with friends rather than on symptoms themselves; stress reduction strategies; individual and/or family therapy to explore sources of anxiety.

Factitious Disorder

Description: Intentional manufacture of physical problems to gain attention, sympathy, assume a sick role, or escape some obligation.

Example: A child has missed a lot of school because of illnesses. One day she complained of stomach pains and wished to go home. You told her to wait a little while to see if she felt any better. You then caught her unobtrusively trying to make herself vomit.

Symptoms: A persistent pattern of deliberately feigned physical symptoms; a personality that is demanding and manipulative; high need for attention.

Usual interventions: Eliminate consequences the child is enjoying as a result of malingering; refer to individual and family therapy to get at sources of need for attention.

Sexual Abuse

Description: The incidence of sexual abuse has been estimated as high as 25% of all girls; although the frequency is less among boys, it is still a major problem; most of these occurrences go unreported and significantly affect a child's self-esteem, development, and school performance.

Example: A child cringes when you softly touch her arm to offer comfort. You have observed that is her usual response to any male who comes too close to her.

Symptoms: Fears of adults, especially own parents; reluctance to go home; withdrawal or regressive behavior; complaints of frequent nightmares; secretiveness about family life; reported stories of being touched inappropriately.

Usual interventions: Suspected sexual abuse must be reported to the authorities, triggering an investigation; treatment usually consists of family therapy, with separate treatment for the perpetrator(s); teachers are instrumental in helping the child develop a safe, trusting relationship with a caring adult; the child is usually seen in individual therapy to work on issues related to betrayal, self-esteem, and accompanying guilt.

Personality Disorders

Description: A relatively enduring, stable set of characteristics that are considered maladaptive. This person usually appears odd (paranoid, schizoid disorders), dramatic and unpredictable (borderline, narcissistic, histrionic, antisocial disorders), or anxious and fearful (avoidant, passive-aggressive, or dependent disorders).

Example: A child has a consistent pattern of lying, theft, truancy, drug abuse, and cruelty to others. He is amoral and irresponsible, responding to nothing that you or anyone else can do to control his behavior.

Symptoms: Behavior on the part of a child that is an extension of his or her personality, self-defeating and quite dysfunctional in daily life.

Usual interventions: The prognosis for these disorders is generally not very good. Because the traits are long-standing and stable, they are resistant to change. These are the children who will consistently give you the most trouble in class. Intensive, long-term individual psychotherapy is usually prescribed, sometimes in addition to group and family therapy. Many times, the teacher will need professional consultation in order to work with these children so that they don't disrupt class functioning.

Adjustment Disorders

Description: Stressful reactions to some recent event in the child's life (such as family death, relocation, illness, or relationship problem).

Example: Formerly a cheerful and very good student, a child became surly, uncooperative, and withdrawn after being informed his parents were getting a divorce. He appeared sad.

Symptoms: Anxiety, depression, withdrawal, behavioral changes, physical complaints, or reduced academic performance immediately following an identifiable stressful event in the child's life.

Usual interventions: These are the kinds of difficulties that respond best to a teacher's empathic concern. The majority of children will improve on their own if provided the time and opportunity to do so. Referral to a counselor can hasten the recovery period, as can participation in support groups. Teachers can often be of tremendous assistance in providing a setting for children to talk about what is bothering them and to feel understood.

Most often, teachers will see this last category of emotional concerns. Fortunately, these emotional concerns are also the kinds of difficulties that respond best to a teacher moderately skilled in helping strategies.

Suggested Activities

1. Do a complete assessment of yourself, including academic, educational, vocational, social, family, and personality factors. Note what you learned from this systematic effort to study your own development. How did this process help you to identify clearer goals for yourself?
2. Interview a partner and attempt to create a comprehensive assessment of his or her strengths and weaknesses in several specific areas. After reviewing your notes, identify several key themes that seemed to emerge. Present the results of this analysis to your partner and then help him or her to process reactions to the feedback.
3. Survey your friends. In what ways could teachers have been more helpful to them while growing up?

Suggested Readings

American Psychiatric Association (1993). *Diagnostic and statistical manual of mental disorders* (4th ed.). Washington, DC: Author.

Kottler, J. A. (1992). *Compassionate therapy: Working with difficult clients.* San Francisco: Jossey-Bass.

Morgan, S. R. (1985). *Children in crisis: A team approach in the schools.* San Diego: College-Hill Press.

Sandoval, J. (1988). *Crisis counseling, intervention, and prevention in the schools.* Hillsdale, NJ: Lawrence Erlbaum.

Seligman, L. (1991). *Selecting effective treatments.* San Francisco: Jossey-Bass.

Thompson, C. L., & Rudolph, L. B. (1992). *Counseling children* (3rd ed.). Pacific Grove, CA: Brooks/Cole.

3

Understanding the
Process of Helping

Once you have been able to assess accurately that a child is in need of help, and perhaps have been able to narrow down the choices to a few reasonable possibilities, you will be ready for the process of helping. In many cases, the appropriate action is to refer the child to a specialist for more expert intervention; in most instances, however, you may very well be able to offer constructive help yourself. What you need to do is follow the systematic process described in this chapter and then apply the skills described in the next chapter.

Counseling Principles

It is not your job to do counseling on a regular basis or to act as a ready confidante for all your students. You will not have the time, opportunity, or training to serve in those roles. But there will be daily instances in which children will reach out to you for understanding, and some rudimentary background in several skills will allow you to help them. First, some basic ideas to keep in mind:

1. *You cannot learn helping skills by reading about them.* If you are serious about augmenting your repertoire of interpersonal skills, you must practice them.

2. *Being in a helping role is NOT natural.* In spite of what you may have heard otherwise, functioning as a counselor means doing a number of things that are *un*natural, such as being non-judgmental and putting your own needs aside.

3. *You are dealing with concerns, not problems.* Problems imply there are solutions, even *right* ones, yet most often personal issues have no single answers. Most of us continue to struggle with our same issues (fear of failure, etc.) our whole lives.

4. *Don't give advice.* By telling people what you think they should do with their lives, one of two things can happen, both of which can lead to negative consequences. First, if you think you know what is best for someone and you tell him what to do, and the results are disastrous, you will get blamed for the rest of your life for being the one at fault. The only thing worse than giving bad advice is giving good advice. If what you tell someone to do works out beautifully, then what they have learned is that when they don't know what to do in the future, they should consult someone else to tell them what to do. You, after all, have reinforced the idea that they are incapable of making decisions on their own.

5. *Don't try to do too much.* The most frequent difficulty that beginning helpers have is, ironically, trying to do too much. Remember, it is the *child's* issue—all you can do is help her feel that she is not alone, that you understand, and that you support her.

6. *Before you begin, slip into a "helping" mode.* Similar to meditation and other altered states of consciousness, helping another person involves focused concentration. When you decide to help someone, you are making a decision, temporarily, to clear your mind of all your own "stuff," to resist distractions, and to stay nonjudgmental about what you are hearing. Furthermore, except when children are in danger of hurting themselves or

someone else, you are committed to keeping private communications confidential.

7. *Don't let yourself feel overwhelmed.* This is only a brief overview of material that would take you three years of full-time study to develop competency in. It is neither realistic nor reasonable for you to expect to put all the ideas and skills presented to use. Our goal is merely to help you expand your current levels of interpersonal effectiveness. As you evolve in your career you will find many opportunities for in-service training, workshops, graduate courses, tapes, and books that will help you become progressively more proficient in these skills.

Helping Attitudes

Although in this and the next chapter we are about to present you with the process and skills of helping, it is important to keep in mind that counseling relationships involve a lot more than mastery of expert techniques. There is a helping attitude that counselors adopt when in session, a state of mind that keeps them clear, focused, and receptive.

We just mentioned being nonjudgmental as one facet of a helping posture. Other features that have been demonstrated again and again as crucial to developing solid relationships are *authenticity, genuineness, caring, respect,* and *compassion.* These are not just words we give lip service to; these attitudes are the essence of what it means to make contact with and truly understand another human being.

Unlike the skills we present, you cannot "learn" these attitudes merely by practicing them. In order to feel caring and compassionate toward children (or anyone), especially when they are going out of their way to be unlovable, you must make a major commitment. Your dedication is obvious because you have already chosen the profession of teaching.

Yet remember that the act of helping is not only an applied set of skills and techniques; it represents your attempt to bring comfort and constructive input to somebody who is struggling or in great pain.

An Integrative Approach to Counseling

You know that educators have long debated which is the best way to promote learning. You have studied dozens of theories, each of which presents an apparently unique explanation to account for how children learn. You have also been exposed to considerable difference of opinion as to the single best way that teachers should operate. You have heard that teachers should concentrate primarily on trying to reinforce and behaviorally manage children's behavior. You have also heard that a developmental, humanistic, or cognitive approach works equally well. The really confusing thing, however, is that all your professors and the authors you've read seem to be right: There are, indeed, a number of conflicting theories of teaching that are all effective even though they rely on supposedly different, even contradictory, principles.

These debates are no less strident in the counseling field. There are as many as 400 different systems of helping that claim that they have evidence indicating that their way of working is the best, that they have discovered "truth." Rather than concentrating on the unique features of different approaches, we focus on the elements that almost all practitioners would agree are important. Any generic helping approach, whether practiced by counselors, psychologists, psychiatrists, social workers, teachers, or witch doctors—whether in our culture, Peru, or Malaysia—will have similar operative ingredients.

Altered States of Consciousness. The object of all helping approaches, whether in teaching or counseling, is to initiate perceptual changes and to influence thinking, feeling, and behavior. Efforts to accomplish these tasks are more likely to be successful if the student is in a receptive mode. This increased receptivity to influence takes place when a person is in a more suggestible mood, a state that can be created by any counselor who constructs a helping environment that is conducive to change. There are things that you can do to increase your status, expertise, and power in children's eyes and thereby help them to be more receptive to what you have to offer.

Placebo Effects. A universal aspect of any change process is influencing children's belief systems in such a way that they become convinced that the procedure will be successful. Doctors do this when they offer relatively benign medications with the accompaniment: "I know this will make you feel better." We do essentially the same thing when we are able to communicate to children that what we do works very well. By believing in our own power to be helpful, we offer hope and inspiration to people who have often given up: "I'm *so* glad you decided to come and speak with me. I have heard a number of children express similar concerns to those that you have mentioned. I have no doubt that you will feel much better after we talk, and I just know that I can help you." This message has an almost hypnotic quality, communicating our belief that the process we offer does indeed work.

Therapeutic Relationship. Of all the universal features that we will mention, the therapeutic relationship may be the most powerful factor of all. Most people strive for intimacy in their lives; each person wishes to be connected to and understood by others. Whereas long ago we all belonged to close knit tribes of friends, relatives, and neighbors who were all concerned with one another, modern life offers a more fragmented, disconnected existence. Children hunger for close relationships, as do adults. One of the common elements of every helping system is an emphasis on creating an alliance that is open, trusting, accepting, and safe. This therapeutic relationship becomes intrinsically healing in some ways. It offers comfort and support. It motivates risk taking. It becomes the core for everything else we do in the helping process.

Cathartic Process. Sigmund Freud discovered long ago that when people are given the opportunity to explore what is bothering them, to talk without interruption about their fears and concerns, they will feel much better afterwards. Every counseling approach has cathartic processes built into it in which the child is permitted and encouraged to talk about whatever is most troublesome. By developing just a few relationship building skills, you will be able to capitalize on these last two elements exceedingly well.

Consciousness Raising. Any significant change means alterations in the way one looks at oneself, at others, and at the world. As teachers, you are particularly well suited to effect these kinds of changes. You are interested in not only increasing children's awareness of the world but also of themselves in relation to others. This element of counseling is thus concerned with promoting more self-understanding and self-discovery, tasks that are certainly within the province of a teacher's role.

Reinforcement. Counseling uses the therapeutic relationship as a means by which to systematically shape more fully functioning behavior and to extinguish self-defeating actions. When the child reports that for the first time she really understands why she has been having certain problems, we offer immediate support; likewise, when she engages in previous maladaptive behavior, we deliberately ignore or discourage those responses. In counseling sessions, this reinforcement may often be quite subtle: As the child speaks of feeling powerful and in control, we smile and nod, whereas when she acts passive and dependent, we appear more neutral and less supportive of this behavior. Of course, the challenge in applying any behavioral principles is to make clear that although we approve and disapprove of certain behavior, we always unconditionally continue to care for the child.

Rehearsal. Counseling sessions provide particularly good opportunities for children to practice new behaviors within the safety of the therapeutic relationship and with plenty of feedback. For example, a child dreads telling his parents that he wants to join the Debate Club instead of trying out for football (a sport he despises), because he thinks they will make fun of him. The teacher helps him rehearse a conversation that he will initiate later that day when his father comes home from work:

Teacher: "Ok, so pretend that I am your Dad. Tell me what you want to say."

Child:	"I don't think I can do this. He just won't listen."
Teacher:	"Are you saying that you don't even want to try?"
Child:	"Well, I guess so."
Teacher:	"You don't sound very convincing."
Child:	"Yes! Yes, I do want to try talking to him."
Teacher:	(Slipping into the role of Father). "So, Son, what did you want to talk to me about?"
Child:	"Um, Dad, I, ah, I just wanted to . . . I mean . . . Oh, never mind."
Teacher:	(Offering support). "Well, that was a start anyway. This time, just say what you want to say. Don't worry how he will respond."

As this coached dialogue continues, the boy is helped to articulate what is most important for him to communicate. He receives feedback on strategies that he might try. Most important, he has the opportunity to practice acting in more powerful ways, an experience that will serve him well in life even if the confrontation with his father does not work out as he would prefer.

Task Facilitation. One of the most important things we can ever do for children is encourage them to try new ways of acting. Most approaches to counseling include helping people complete therapeutic tasks. Obviously, the child in the previous example has a tremendous amount of reluctance to speaking with his father. If we can define a successful outcome as not so much getting one's way as trying to act courageously, then the child will feel better about himself no matter how his father responds to his overture.

*   *   *

Each preceding element just reviewed is part of all counseling efforts, regardless of the theoretical persuasion of the practitioner. As we look in greater depth at exactly what is involved in a counseling encounter with a child, keep in mind that this is a "generic" approach, one that most members of the profession would agree is somewhat universal. As you come to gain more experience and training, you may very well adapt this general approach to one that fits better with your personality, teaching style, and student population.

A Review of the Counseling Process

The counseling process follows a series of logical and sequential stages, not unlike what you might invent intuitively from any problem-solving effort. Although these components are presented as if they were discrete parts, in fact the boundaries often overlap to the point where it's hard to determine which stage you're at. The important point is to have an overview of how helping takes place, the stages that children usually go through, and a blueprint for where you are headed once you identify your current position in the process.

Assessment. Before you can attempt any effort at being helpful you have to have some idea as to what is going on. Counselors and therapists call this the "identification of the presenting complaint," but actually it is simply a systematic effort to help the child describe what is bothersome. It is also crucial to collect any important background information relevant to the child's concerns.

As you imagine yourself conducting this assessment, it will probably occur to you that there are a number of skills you would need that are probably not already part of your professional repertoire. The next chapter reviews in greater detail the particular skills required, but for now we will simply indicate which skills are important in the various stages. To begin, the counseling skills most often associated with an assessment are (1) asking questions, (2) reflecting the child's feelings, and (3) clarifying the content of what is being presented.

Imagine that a child tells you he is upset because he doesn't have many friends. Immediately, you would think of a number of questions you want to ask; you need more information in order to be helpful to this person: What do you mean you don't have many friends? Who *are* you close to? What have you tried to do so far to resolve this difficulty? When you are feeling down, what do you do about it? Who knows about this concern of yours? What do you hope that I can do to help you? By using reflective skills that encourage the child to elaborate on what he has presented, you will find that these questions rarely need to be asked directly. Eventually, both you and the child will have a clearer idea of what the child is struggling with, and with which part of the problem he most wants assistance.

Exploration. Once you have identified the "presenting complaint," the next logical step is to dig deeper into what is going on, to discover how this concern is related to the child's life. You will continue to use reflective skills to help him clarify what he is feeling and thinking. Applying the skill of "advanced level empathy" will help him get at the hidden, disguised, and subtle nuances of his experience. Empathy means that you are able to get inside someone else's skin to the point that you can sense what he or she is going through. In this exploration stage you will use your sensitivity and understanding of the child's experience to help him move to deeper levels of awareness.

The boy without friends might be helped to explore the depth of his feelings of loneliness and estrangement from others. He would become aware of how much he misses having close friends, how much he wishes he could change his situation. With probing from his teacher, he also articulates some of the anger he feels toward his parents for moving him away from his old neighborhood where he had been perfectly content. Prior to this conversation, he had never been able to say out loud how much he still grieved the loss of his old friends and how resentful he still felt for being pulled away without his consent.

Understanding. The deeper the exploration of one's feelings and thoughts, the more profound the insights that are generated as a result of this process. The helper, at this point, uses more active skills such as confrontation, interpretation, self-disclosure, and the giving of information to help the child understand his own role in creating his difficulty. Furthermore, insights are typically generated around understanding why and how the problem developed, what the child is doing to sabotage himself from improving, and what themes are being repeated over and over in his life.

The lonely child is confronted with the realization that his prior life was not as wonderful as he makes it out to be. In fact, he was also lonely in his old neighborhood; the only reason it seemed like he had more friends was because there were more children around the immediate vicinity of his home. He still had not been close to many others. He, therefore, began to accept more responsibility for his own plight. He looked at his fears of being rejected and his strategies of scaring other people away before they had the chance to reject him. He also learned about the self-defeating ways in which he stopped himself from initiating more relationships: He would tell himself negative things and exaggerate the consequences of what could go wrong if somebody did not want to play with him. Finally, his teacher helped him to understand that he did have the power to change this whole pattern of his life if only he were willing to take some risks and try some new ways of acting.

Action. Although understanding and insight are wonderful things, without action to change one's behavior they are useless. There are many people walking around this earth who understand, with perfect clarity, why they are so messed up, but they refuse to do anything to change their ways. The action stage of helping is thus geared to helping children translate what they know and understand into a plan that will get them what they want.

The first part of this action process involves establishing goals that the child wishes to reach. Next, using a variety of skills ranging from problem solving to role-playing, the teacher helps the child generate a list of viable alternative courses of action, to narrow them down to those that seem most realistic and attractive, and then to make a commitment to follow through on one's intentions.

The lonely boy is helped to clarify exactly what he would like to be able to do that he is unable or unwilling to do—most notably (1) initiate new relationships, (2) overcome his fears of rejection, and (3) stop doing things that tend to drive people away. He is helped to define more specifically what these goals mean, in other words, to break down in smaller steps what it means to initiate relationships or what specific things he is prone to doing that turn people off. He is then helped to digest small bite-size pieces of his ultimate goal, slowly making incremental progress. He might start out initiating a pleasant exchange with someone in his class or sharing his dessert during lunch, for example. From there, he might eventually work up to asking someone new if he could join him or her for lunch. After practicing these realistic tasks that he would assign to himself, he would be able to invite someone over to his house to play, and more important, not be devastated if they could not or would not come.

Evaluation. The final stage in the helping process involves evaluating with the child the extent to which he or she has reached desired goals. This systematic assessment of progress helps you measure the impact of your interventions and helps the child take inventory of what has been accomplished as well as what is left to do.

Because as a teacher there are limits to the time and opportunities you have to guide a child all the way through this process, referral will play an important part of your helping effort. If you can do nothing else, you want children to have had a good experience talking to you so that they will be more inclined to take your direction when you urge them to seek additional help.

One struggling student, for example, did make considerable progress in overcoming her reluctance to reach out to others. More important, the teacher helped her to clarify her feelings about her plight and accept responsibility that it was more something that she was doing to herself rather than something that was being done to her.

In addition to her social shyness, this girl also had some other difficulties such as a low frustration tolerance, a nonsupportive home life, and a history of giving up when things didn't go her way. Because of these complications, progress became erratic though certainly noticeable. The teacher realized that she neither had the time nor the inclination to work on a deeper level with the child. He therefore decided in his evaluative process with her that she needed more help than he could offer. He addressed her reluctance to start over with someone else and reassured her that he would still be available in a supportive capacity. The child was then receptive to accepting the suggestion that she consult with the school counselor and work out with him whether that setting or one in the community would be the best place for her to continue working on herself.

The Link Between the Counseling Process and Helping Skills

Now that you have an understanding of the "big picture" of functioning in a counseling role with a child, you can appreciate that you will need a number of skills to capitalize on therapeutic elements and to move through the sequential stages of helping. Although we have mentioned that certain skills, such as questioning and reflecting, are usually linked to the assessment and exploration stages, in reality you will use almost all of the different counselor behaviors in all phases of your helping efforts.

Suggested Activities

1. Define how a professional helping relationship is different from a relationship with friends.
2. Think of an unresolved issue in your life. Apply the steps of the counseling process to work yourself through (a) an assessment of the issue, (b) an understanding of the underlying themes and connected issues, (c) an action plan of what you propose to do, and (d) how you intend to evaluate the results of your effort.
3. Being nonjudgmental and accepting are important elements in the helping process. Identify several subjects that may come up in conversations with children about which you feel very strongly (abortion, drug use, sexual

activity, discrimination, and so on). Imagine a child expresses values that are the antithesis of your own. Formulate responses that would avoid imposing a critical, judgmental attitude.

Suggested Readings

Basch, M. (1988). *Understanding psychotherapy.* New York: Basic Books.

Corey, G. (1990). *Theory and practice of counseling and psychotherapy.* Pacific Grove, CA: Brooks/Cole.

Kottler, J. A. (1991). *The compleat therapist.* San Francisco: Jossey-Bass.

Meier, S. T. (1989). *The elements of counseling.* Pacific Grove, CA: Brooks/Cole.

Developing Skills of Helping

Although the focus of our discussion now turns to the *skills* of relating to children in a helpful capacity, much of your success in these endeavors will depend on things you do inside your own head before the conversation even starts. Counseling encounters, you see, are different than normal human interactions because of the helper's state of mind as he or she enters the relationships. Counseling is, in a way, a form of meditation in which both participants are concentrating intently on what the other is saying; it is as if nothing or nobody else exists outside the circle of their interaction.

Counselors and therapists often are accused of being able to read minds when, in fact, what they are doing is simply focusing all their attention, all their energy, their very being, on what the other person is saying, doing, and meaning by their words or gestures. With such full and complete attention toward others, it is indeed possible to anticipate what they will say next and even what they are thinking, even though they haven't fully articulated these ideas to themselves.

Before you begin a counseling encounter, it is thus extremely important to take steps to clear your mind of all distractions, to put aside your own worries, your grumbling stomach, the tasks you must complete later in the day. In yoga, meditation, martial arts, or any contemplative art (of which counseling is certainly a part), participants are encouraged to take a "cleansing breath" before they begin their activity. A deep breath helps clear yourself of muddled and distracting thoughts and helps "center" yourself on the interaction that is about to begin. This breath comes to symbolize the commitment that you are making to the child, that for the next few minutes nothing exists except your interest and caring for him or her. If you experiment with this kind of attitude in other relationships in your life, you will notice a remarkable change taking place in the quality and intimacy of your interactions.

Once you have cleared your mind and focused your concentration, it is next imperative that you monitor your internal attitudes. Counselors are helpful precisely because they are perceived as being nonjudgmental, accepting, and noncritical. Whereas outside the helping encounter you could quite easily feel critical toward what you are hearing, once you have made a decision to function in a helping role, you are making a decision to suspend, temporarily, that part of you that judges others; judgments interfere with your ability to respond compassionately to what you are hearing. If the child senses even a little bit of authoritarian criticism on your part, all trust can be lost.

In this initial stage of making contact with a child, before you even open your mouth to say anything or apply your first helping skill, you are already setting in motion an internal state of mind, a set of helping attitudes, to help yourself be maximally receptive and responsive to what you will hear. You are reminding yourself to stay flexible, to push aside distractions, and to feel compassionate toward what is about to take place.

Attending

Easier than it may sound, appearing attentive to children is the first and most basic task in being helpful. If you would simply monitor yourself and others during most interactions, you would notice how rare it is that people are being fully attentive to one another. While addressing you, and purportedly listening, a friend is also probably engaged in a number of simultaneous activities—looking over your shoulder, waving to someone walking by, rustling through papers, grooming hair. Such divided behavior hardly inspires your confidence, nor does it communicate that you are all that important to that person during that moment in time.

Attending to someone means giving them your total, complete, undivided interest. It means using your body, your face, your eyes, yes, especially your eyes, to say: "Nothing exists right now for me except you. Every ounce of my energy and being is focused on you."

You would be truly amazed at how healing this simple act can be—giving another person your full attention. Children, in particular, are often so used to being devalued by adults that attending behaviors instantly tell them something is different about this interaction: "Here is a person who seems to care about me and what I have to say."

Listening

Attending skills involve the use of nonverbal behaviors (head nods, smiles, eye contact, body positions) and minimal verbal encouragement ("uh-huh," "I see") to communicate our intense interest in what a person is saying. Although these skills are a requirement to earn a person's trust, they are relatively empty gestures unless you are actually listening and can prove that you have understood.

This presents an interesting challenge: How do you demonstrate to people that you understand them? How do you show them that you not only heard what they said, but you really know what they mean?

There are two ways to show evidence of such synchronized attention: *passive listening*, which we have already described in the context of nonverbal and verbal attending, and *active listening* in which you take a more direct role in responding to what you heard. Ultimately, listening is communicated by the way you respond to the speaker, by your ability to prove that you really did hear what has been said.

Empathic Resonance

Empathy is the ability (and willingness) to crawl inside someone else's skin and to know what he or she is experiencing. This is where attending, listening, and interpersonal sensitivity come together in such a way that you are able to get outside yourself enough so that you can sense what the other person is feeling and thinking.

The second part of this helping behavior involves communicating your understanding of what you hear/see/sense/feel in such a way that the child does not feel quite so alone.

At its most basic level, beginning counselors are taught to use the stem "You feel_____" to respond to each client statement. Although this may sound artificial and contrived, it does help to get one in the habit of focusing on and resonating with a child's "felt experience."

Let's put together these first three skills into a dialogue with a student who is upset about a poor grade she received on an exam:

Student: "You gave me a D on this test." (Said accusingly, with tears in her eyes.)

Teacher: Puts down papers she was grading. Turns her chair to face the student fully. Softens her face and waits patiently [attending]. "Yes, that's true. You did earn a D on the exam." [Note the way the statement is reworded—placing emphasis on student's responsibility.]

Student: "Well, I don't think that's right! This test wasn't fair."

Teacher: Nods head [attending]. "You don't think the test covered the stuff you had prepared for." [Active listening.]

Student: "Well, it didn't. And now my parents will kill me."

Teacher: "You sound more concerned about your parents'
             reaction than you do about the test itself." [Empathic
             resonance.]

Student: "They just expect so much from me."

Teacher: Nods her head [attending]. Smiles reassuringly [pas-
             sive listening]. "Yes, I can see how difficult this is for
             you. You are really feeling under a lot of pressure."
             [Empathic resonance.]

As is evident from this helping encounter, these first counseling skills are connected to one another in that they all attempt
to build an open, trusting, and accepting atmosphere in which
the student will feel comfortable disclosing and exploring her
feelings.

Exploration Skills

Questioning

Certainly the most obvious and direct way to gather information or encourage children to explore a particular area is to ask
them a series of questions. As you read the previous dialogue
probably a number of ideas came to mind: Why do you feel the
test was unfair? How much time did you study for the test?
How are you doing in your other classes? What will your
parents do when they find out? What do your parents expect of
you? And so on.

The problem with questions, as natural as they may come to
mind, is that they often put the child in a "one down" position
in which you are the interrogator and expert problem solver.
"Tell me what the situation is and I will fix it." For that reason,
questions are used only when you can't get the student to reveal
information in other ways. You would be amazed at how much
territory you can cover by relying on other, more indirect methods of exploration.

If you must ask questions, word them in such a way that they
are "open-ended," or the kind that can't be answered with a

single word, rather than "close-ended," those that can be satisfied with a one-word response. Contrast the differences in the examples below:

Open-ended	*Close-ended*
What are you feeling right now?	Are you feeling upset?
What are you going to do?	Are you going to tell your parents?

It is fairly obvious that open-ended questions encourage further exploration, whereas close-ended queries tend to cut off communication. You may have the answer to your question but at the expense of prolonged silence in which the child is waiting for you to continue directing the course of the conversation.

One notable exception to the rule of avoiding questions whenever possible, especially close-ended ones, is when it is important to gather very specific information in a potentially threatening or dangerous situation. If a child, for example, expressed suicidal fantasies, it would in that case be very appropriate to ask specific questions: "Have you ever tried it before? Do you have a plan for how you would do it? Do you have the means to carry out your plan? Will you promise me not to do anything at all until we can get you some help?" A "yes" response to the first three questions and "no" to the last would signal the need to take some definite preventive action beyond the scope of merely reflecting the child's feelings.

Reflecting Content

An indirect way to help someone further explore his or her concerns is to use your listening and empathy skills to reflect the content of what he or she is saying. This does not mean you should sound like a parrot, but rather it indicates that by *rewording* you have heard accurately what was said. These restatements help people to clarify further what they are saying and facilitate additional exploration into the issues.

| Child: | "Mikey keeps hitting me. He won't leave me alone and teases me all of the time." |
| Teacher: | "Mikey won't get off your back no matter what you do." |

In this simple reflection of content, the teacher acknowledges what was heard and also guides the focus toward the child's own behavior ("no matter what *you* do").

Reflecting Feelings

This skill is quite similar to the previous one but has a different emphasis: on feelings rather than content. The intent here is to identify and reflect the underlying feelings that you hear expressed in a young person's statements. Although this may, at first, seem like an easy thing to do, it is among the most complex and difficult tasks that counselors undertake. To reflect feelings sensitively, accurately, and helpfully, you must to be able to (l) listen very carefully to subtle nuances of what is being said, (2) decode the deeper meanings of communication, (3) identify accurately the feelings a person is experiencing, and (4) communicate this understanding in a way that it can be accepted.

Child:	"My friends think I should talk to you."
Teacher:	"You're feeling pressured by your friends, but a part of you needs to talk about something bothering you." (Note the first part reflects the content, the second part identifies the apprehension.)
Child:	"Yeah, I do need to talk about this, I guess." (Silence.)
Teacher:	"It's hard for you to do this." (Even silence can be reflected.)
Child:	(Deep breath) "Here goes. My girlfriend wants to have sex, and I guess I do, too, but . . . ."
Teacher:	"You are supposed to want to have sex. You are the guy. Yet, you also don't feel ready just yet."
Child:	"Any guy would want to sleep with Karen. Me, too. My friends think I'm nuts. But, I just think that sex should, well, you know . . . . "
Teacher:	"It's just more complicated for you than a simple act. You feel excited, apprehensive, and a little overwhelmed."

And so continues a dialogue in which the teacher relies on reflection of feeling to help the adolescent explore his deeper feelings, to help him clarify what he really wants, and eventually to help him resolve what *he* wants to do—to make his own decision—apart from pressures from his girlfriend, his friends, family, and even the teacher. It is through such an exchange that it is possible for children to find out what *they* truly believe in and act on those convictions.

Self-Disclosure

This is the skill in which you demonstrate authenticity, genuineness, and humanness to children. Idealizing us as they sometimes do, it may be helpful for them to hear the ways that we have struggled with similar issues (if that is the case) and to connect with us on an intimate level.

As this intervention has the potential for abuse (talking about yourself too much, too often, at inappropriate times, or revealing inappropriate material), self-disclosure should be concise, devoid of self-indulgence, and used *very* conservatively. The danger is that by revealing too much about yourself, you will violate professional boundaries, reveal information about yourself that could be damaging, or focus too much on yourself.

Self-disclosures are best when you are showing the child is not alone, bridging perceived distance between you, and modeling openness.

Teacher: "I know what you are going through. My parents were divorced also and I struggled for quite a while before I got my feet back on the ground."

Another variety of self-disclosure, called *immediacy*, involves sharing what you are feeling about the interaction or what you are feeling toward the child at a particular moment in time:

Teacher: "I really feel honored that you decided to trust me. I feel closer to you after what you've told me. And, I respect you for your courage."

Summarizing

Used at least once at the end of any conversation, but which can be inserted any time a wrap-up is needed, the summary ties together themes that were discussed and puts things in perspective. Ideally, the teacher can summarize *after* having asked the child to do so first, "So, what are you leaving with?" The teacher can then fill in the gaps.

Teacher: "I agree that we have helped you clarify your beliefs about sex and some aspects of your relationship with Karen. In addition, however, we looked at your desire to think for yourself more often instead of simply following the lead of others. You said you wished to tell your friends to respect your wishes and stop trying to push you. And you want to sit down with Karen and tell her how you feel."

A good summary logically provides a transition between the exploration phase of helping and the action strategies for making needed changes.

Action Skills

Your role as a teacher will limit the action strategies you can employ. This will be frustrating for you because the one thing you will want to do—and that all beginners try to do—is to jump in and fix the problem—or at least fix what you *think* is the problem.

Most often, your helping role will be to listen, to understand, to communicate empathy as you're helping the child to clarify what the issues are. Then, you will refer the child for appropriate professional help

At times, however, you will have the opportunity to help the child convert what has been discussed into some constructive action. The following skills are thus described to you with a note of caution: Get more training and supervision before you attempt any intrusive means of intervention. That especially includes giving advice, the single most abused helping strategy.

Advice Giving

Don't do it. Period. Resist your natural inclination to tell people what to do with their lives. Are you sure you know what is best for anyone else? Do you really know what is best for you? Are you sure you want the responsibility that comes with telling someone else what to do?

The exceptions to this prohibition take place only when children are tempted to do something that is potentially dangerous to themselves or others. Then you are not only permitted but *required* to do something. Remember, however, that the *way* you offer advice will determine the extent to which a child is likely to pay attention and follow your words of wisdom.

Teacher: "I think that before you take such a drastic step, you should talk to some people first. Tell your friends, only the ones you trust, what you have in mind. Hear what they have to say. Then let's talk again."

Goal Setting

This is the consummate action skill, the one that satisfies both you and your student's need to translate some elusive, ambiguous issue into concrete results. Unlike dreaded homework assignments, however, this kind of goal is definitely not prescribed by you—many children already may feel resentment toward teachers for telling them what to do. Instead, you will take the longer more laborious route of helping children define and follow through on their own stated goals—that way, they are much more likely to complete them. And, even if they don't do what they said they would, you can unconcernedly shrug and say, "Oh, well, I guess you didn't want to do it after all." Then when the student replies, "But I did! I *did* want to do it. I just didn't have time," you can smile and reply, "Fine. You'll do it when you want."

There are other factors to keep in mind when helping people to set goals for themselves:

1. Make sure the goal they identify is really related to the central issue they are struggling with. Losing 10 pounds may be a very good thing to do, but if one's weight isn't the major impediment to high self-esteem, then efforts could be wasted.

2. Construct goals that are realistic and attainable. A student enthusiastic to change can become overzealous, naively believing he can do everything overnight. Help students take small, manageable steps, ensuring they will experience success in their efforts. A child who has few friends, for example, could start with carrying on two-minute-long conversations with others before undertaking progressively more difficult tasks.

3. Whenever possible, make the goals as specific as possible. Include *what* the person will do, *where* he or she will do it, *when* and *how often* it will be done, *for how long* it will be continued, *with whom, who* will be present, and *what contingencies* will be in place if he or she should falter. These factors can help translate a student's imprecise concerns into action goals. For example:

Before: "I get in fights a lot. I want to stop but other kids sometimes push me too far. I let them do that. I also know that I can't keep fighting all the time or I won't have any friends left. No teeth either. So, I guess what I have to do is stop fighting so much."

After: "Between now and tomorrow at this time I will not get in a single *physical* fight with anyone at school. (I can't guarantee what might happen at home with my brothers.) If I should start to lose my temper during the next day at school, I will repeat to myself what we talked about. If that doesn't work too well, I give you my word, no, I mean I promise to *myself* that I will walk away. If I absolutely have to defend myself I will only do so with my mouth, not my fists."

As can be seen, this young man's goal for the next 24 hours meets the criteria described earlier. Sometimes, you can make a tremendous difference in a person's life by having them talk things out and decide what they want to do, then help them to create a plan for how they can get what they want.

Problem Solving

A more elaborate version of goal setting, involving a sequential series of steps, is applying a problem-solving approach to a student's difficulties. Assume, for example, that a student wants to go to college but doesn't have the financial means or an academic track record that would qualify her for a scholarship. The student feels frustrated and hopeless, ready to give up the dream and resolve herself to menial, repetitive work.

Any problem-solving strategy would (1) help define the problem; (2) specify the goals; (3) develop alternatives that might be constructive; (4) narrow the choices to those that seem most realistic; and (5) put the plan into action.

With the help of her teacher, the student generated a surprisingly long list of possibilities, ranging from going to summer school, to getting a tutor, to finding a better-paying job, to going to a community college, to working for a while after graduation to save money before going to college, to joining the military to earn college tuition. After limiting the choices to the few that seemed most appealing, the student was able to target her energy on a specific plan that was quite within her reach.

Reframing

Imagine a nice picture in an ugly frame, one that so detracts from the art that it loses its lustre and appeal. Take the same picture, put it in a different frame, and *voila!*—a true thing of beauty! That is the analogy of reframing in a helping context.

A most creative, challenging, and fun endeavor, reframing is a skill difficult to learn. It is a way of thinking about things that people present to you in a completely different light. Your task is to take a problem that someone describes, usually one that you can do absolutely nothing about, and then reframe it in such a way that solutions more readily suggest themselves. In its most basic mode, you take what the student has said—"I'm stupid" (a predicament that if it *were* true, you could do little to help)—and then alter it in such a way that it appears more easily resolvable: "You are less talented than you would like to be in quantitative subjects, but you are quite brilliant at drawing funny pictures and fixing things that are broken. That doesn't sound like someone who is stupid to me."

Some other examples of reframing in action:

Statement	Reframing
"I'm shy."	"You act shyly when you are in new situations without your close friends around."
"I hate school."	"You don't enjoy structured learning very much, but you really do like school when you have freedom to do what you want."
"My child says that all his teachers say he is disruptive. My child is *not* disruptive."	"Your child has a great sense of humor. He is just performing for the wrong audience."
"Your lectures are boring."	"You find it hard to concentrate on content presentations."

In each case, the teacher seeks to reframe the definition of the problem in a more optimistic light. Sometimes this works; sometimes it doesn't. As with all helping efforts, we try a variety of approaches until we find the right combination.

Cognitive Restructuring

Reframing is a cognitive intervention that helps people shift the way they view their concerns. Other techniques help children think differently about their plights, the most popular of which are known as rational-emotive therapy developed by Albert Ellis and cognitive therapy developed by Aaron Beck.

The theory behind these techniques is quite simple: What we feel is based on how we think about what is happening. If we change the way we interpret a predicament, we can thus change how we feel about it. Our job, then, is to teach children to realize they have choices about how they can react to events in their lives. Very little is intrinsically bad or annoying or frustrating. It is our perception of these experiences that determine our reactions. "If you don't like how you are feeling," the cognitive therapist says, "then change how you feel about it!"

This approach to helping should be exciting to you for a number of reasons. First, it is easily learned, and with a little practice you will find yourself becoming more and more skilled at helping people understand that the way they think about their problems determines, to a great extent, how they subsequently feel and behave. Second, this is a problem-solving approach that you can apply immediately to your own life. In fact, the more you work on your own internal thinking patterns, the more proficient you will be in helping others with theirs. Likewise, the more you practice helping children confront their irrational beliefs and illogical thoughts, the more you will notice profound changes in your own personal effectiveness. Third, and most exciting of all, using these cognitive strategies can make a difference in a child's life in a very short period of time.

The process of cognitive helping follows a fairly logical sequence in which you first help a student to articulate the feelings that are bothersome. The helping skills mentioned earlier (active listening, reflections of feeling, open-ended questioning) are often useful.

Teacher: "What exactly are you feeling right now?"
Student: "I don't know. Just kind of upset."
Teacher: "You're feeling down about something."
Student: "Yes, I'm down alright. But I'm also really mad!"
Teacher: "I can see that. You sure seem angry. But also hurt."

So far, the teacher has helped the student identify four different feelings she is experiencing—upset, down, mad, and hurt. With more time, the list could be lengthened even further because usually we feel many different things when we are upset about something.

Next, the student would be encouraged to describe the particular situation that she believes is causing her the problems. At this juncture, the student describes what exactly took place.

Teacher: "Tell me what happened."
Student: "Oh, you know, that dumb play I tried out for."
Teacher: "You didn't do as well as you hoped, huh?"
Student: "You can say that again. I didn't even get called back for another reading."

So the incident that the student feels has "ruined her life forever" is not getting a part in a play.

Because the point of this helping procedure is that other people or events don't make you feel anything—you make yourself feel things based on how you think—the next step is to help the student identify the internal thoughts or irrational beliefs that are creating the suffering. This part is a bit tricky because it requires you to be familiar with the main themes prevalent in irrational thinking. Basically, irrational beliefs fall into three main groups:

1. *Exaggerations of reality.* People make things seem much worse than they really are by distorting the significance of what took place: "Because I didn't get the part in the play, I'll never do what I want in life." Or: "Everyone will laugh at me when they find out."

2. *Demands that the world be different.* This set of irrational beliefs results from expectations that the world or people be different than they are. We set ourselves up as special beings who deserve special attention. Common manifestations of this irrational thinking usually begin with the pronouncement:

"It's not fair	. . . that I didn't get what I want."
	. . . that he treated me that way."
	. . . that the rules were changed."

This thinking is irrational because, clearly, the world is not fair. We are *not* entitled to special attention. And just because we have certain expectations for people, it does not mean they are obligated to live up to them.

3. *Judging oneself in absolute terms.* This is a variation of the previous irrational thinking in which you apply unrealistic or perfectionistic standards to yourself that you could never live up to. For example:

- "Because I didn't perform as well as I would like in this situation, I will never be good at this, or anything."
- "Because I got a D on this exam, I am stupid."
- "Because she won't go out with me, I'll never meet anyone I like who likes me back."

Words like "must," "should," and "never" are cues we are making demands of ourselves that are self-imposed and probably not realistic.

Even with this thumbnail sketch of irrational themes, you have some idea of how the teacher could move the child to the last and most important stage—challenging those irrational beliefs and confronting their veracity. These interventions require that you are able to apply cognitive techniques to yourself before you can work successfully with others. In other words, you can't talk people into letting go of their dysfunctional thinking unless you can dispute your own.

In the case we have been following, the dialogue might develop as follows:

Teacher: "So what you are saying is that because you didn't get this part in the play, you are a worthless person?"

Student: "Yup."

Teacher: "And that makes sense to you? Listen to yourself."

Student: "But I wanted that part so badly."

Teacher: "I understand that. The part that makes no sense is that you are saying that because you wanted something very badly and didn't get it this one time, it means that everything you did before doesn't matter, and everything you will do in the future is ruined."

Student: "Ok. So maybe I exaggerated a little. But you have to agree that the whole audition was a crock."

Teacher: "Let's assume that you are right: It wasn't fair. So what?"

Student: "Huh?"

Teacher: "Since when are auditions fair and impartial?"

Student: "But they should be fair! I mean . . ."

Teacher: "That's not the point. I agree with you. And after this, let's talk about what you could do to change the system. But for now, why are you so surprised the selection process isn't fair? This isn't the first time you have encountered favoritism in the selection process.

"Look, you can't change what happened, but you can change the way you think about it. The only thing worse than not getting the part, is not getting the part *and then* making yourself miserable for days afterwards."

This interaction gives you a flavor of the rich opportunities available to teach children to feel more control over their internal states. Children feel so little power in their lives that it is especially exciting to introduce them to a way of thinking that allows them to decide how they want to feel about things.

The "map" on the next page highlights the strategy in which children are challenged to:

1. Accept greater responsibility for their thoughts and feelings.
2. Be more aware of what is going on inside their heads.
3. Become more analytical and logical in the ways they reason through cause-effect relationships.
4. Make choices about how they want to react to the things and people around them.
5. Change the ways they feel by altering the ways they think.

The teacher closes her talk with the student by reinforcing these very ideas:

"It is no wonder you were upset. It wasn't only a matter of not getting the part, but also the way you reacted to that situation. It is understandable that you would be disappointed, but not so down that you can barely function— that you did to yourself. Any time in the future you don't like the way you are feeling, you can follow this same procedure of figuring out what you are saying to yourself about the event and then change your internal thoughts."

The object of these confrontations is to help a person realize the extent of his or her distortions and substitute more realistic and appropriate responses. Confrontations come in other forms as well.

The whole process we just went through is reviewed in the chart below:

MAP OF COGNITIVE INTERVENTIONS

A The Incident	B Irrational Belief	C Resulting Emotions	D Disputing Irrational Beliefs
"I didn't get the part in the play."	1. "This isn't fair!" 2. "I'll never get what I want."	upset depressed hurt shame anger	1. "True, life isn't fair. So what?" 2. "Just because I didn't get this part doesn't mean I am not a good person, or even a good actor."
	3. "Everyone will laugh."		3. "Not everyone will laugh. Some people may laugh, but they aren't the people I care about."
	4. "This is the worst thing that could happen to me."		4. "This is only a minor setback."

Confrontations

There are times when people need to hear they have crossed a boundary or when they need to understand the discrepancies between what they are doing and what they said they want, or what they are saying now versus what they said earlier. The secret is to confront someone in such a way that he or she will not feel defensive.

The best confrontations are thus presented neutrally, matter-of-factly, even tentatively, as if to say that you have noticed something interesting that they might find helpful: "Gee, I'm confused. You are saying that you want good grades in school, yet you mentioned earlier that you never study."

You are putting the observation before children and letting them decide what they want to do about it. This is, obviously, the most intrusive of interventions and, hence, the one that must be applied most cautiously and carefully. You can as easily alienate or wound someone deeply with a mistimed or insensitive confrontation as you can help facilitate a major breakthrough. The key, therefore, before attempting any confrontation, is to ask yourself whether you are offering this intervention out of caring for the other person or whether it represents an attempt to be punitive or to put the person down.

Encouragement

We saved the best for last. Children experience certain concerns for which there are no easy solutions and which you can do little about except offer support. Encouragement is listed here as an "action" skill because it is a deliberate and intentional effort on your part to foster hope in those who are without it.

Imagine a child who finds out she has leukemia, or another whose father died in a hunting accident, or still another whose parents are separating, or one who just found out she will be moving out of state. What would you propose to do in these situations? The answer, of course, is that your act of doing is really one of encouragement.

You communicate, in effect, that you have complete confidence that the child will indeed recover a positive state of mind. Furthermore, you intend to be there for him or her along the way. Because you believe in the child's power and strength, he or she will regain a sense of balance. Sometimes, your support is all that you have to give.

Suggested Activities

1. Find a partner to work with and practice the skills mentioned in this chapter. Start with basic attending skills:
   (a) Carry on a conversation with your partner in which neither of you maintains eye contact; then, after a few minutes, concentrate on making good eye contact; notice the difference.
   (b) Continue your conversation but with both of you showing blank expressions on your faces; after a few minutes, both of you show animation, warmth, and expressiveness in your face; notice the difference.
   (c) As you continue your talk, add to these attending skills a more concerted effort on your part to use head nods, "uh-huhs," and other acknowledgments that you are following and understanding what your partner is saying; notice the effect.
2. Choose a partner to work with. One of you decide to be the "client" first while the other of you will be the "helper." The client should play the role of a child who feels left out of activities during recess and wants to stay inside with the teacher. The helper should *only* respond with active listening skills, primarily restatements and reflections of feeling.
3. With a partner you can practice asking open-ended questions that encourage rather than cut off communication. Each of you write down three questions that you believe will elicit maximum information from your partner and encourage him or her to examine important issues. Ask your questions of one another and note their effectiveness.

4. Concentrate on a few of the skills presented in this chapter and make them part of the normal way you relate to others. Find opportunities every day in which you can practice your new skills. Report to your peers the ways in which you are aware there are differences in your interpersonal style.

5. Recruit the assistance of an expert who can observe you applying the skills in this chapter (or record an interview on tape). Ask for specific feedback on ways you could improve your performance.

6. Select an incident in your life about which you feel some lingering distress. Apply the cognitive intervention strategy presented in this chapter to help yourself:

   (a) Label what you are feeling
   (b) Identify the irrational beliefs and distorted interpretations that are creating your suffering
   (c) Dispute the irrational beliefs

   Write down each stage of the process. Make a commitment to incorporate this way of processing emotional discomfort into your life by practicing several times each day.

Suggested Readings

Cormier, W. H., & Cormier, L. S. (1991). *Interviewing strategies for helpers.* Pacific Grove, CA: Brooks/Cole.

Egan, G. (1990). *The skilled helper* (4th ed.). Pacific Grove, CA: Brooks/Cole.

Evans, D. R., Hearn, M. T., Uhlemann, M. R., & Ivey, A. E. (1989). *Essential interviewing: A programmed approach to effective communication* (3rd ed.). Pacific Grove, CA: Brooks/Cole.

Gazda, G. M., Asbury, F. R., Childers, W. C., & Walters, R. P. (1991). *Human relations development: A manual for educators* (4th ed.). Boston: Allyn & Bacon.

Helping Strategies in Groups

You can apply the skills of helping in settings other than individual conferences. Although there is no substitute for the intimacy and focused attention of being with a child in private, it is often impractical to find both the time and opportunity to do so in light of everything else that infringes on your time—papers to grade, lessons to prepare, meetings to attend—already more than you can handle comfortably. Working with children in groups is an alternative way to help many children deal with troublesome issues, especially if you can adjust the usual ways you run your classroom.

Differences Between Process and Classroom Groups

Most of your training in group leadership has been designed to help you present information and assess the degree to which children have learned this material. Thus you are prepared to give lectures, use audio-visual aids in your presentations, devise projects for students to work on in groups, divide the class into study groups for cooperative learning, and play team games with children.

In contrast, process-oriented groups provide different kinds of educational experiences for children. Specifically, these growth-oriented experiences differ from the usual classroom instruction in the following ways:

The emphasis is not on content. There is no specific information that you wish students to learn in process groups. Your intent, instead, is to provide a safe environment in which children may explore their own values, feelings, and beliefs about themselves, about others, and about their experiences.

Participants are encouraged to share their own personal reactions to ideas rather than ideas themselves. Unlike the usual classroom activities that focus on intellectual ideas or the development of skills, process groups require participants to speak about their very personal reactions to what they have experienced and are experiencing.

Small talk, rambling, and focus on outsiders is not permitted. It is crucial to keep attention on what is taking place in the group. You do not let children complain about what others are doing, nor do you let them ramble, intellectualize, or engage in meaningless prattle; you keep them focused on what they are feeling and thinking. You make sure that time is equitably distributed among all children.

Process groups are student-centered rather than teacher-centered. In many classroom arrangements the teacher stands before the class presenting content. All eyes and ears in the room are supposed to be attending to this one person, clearly the most important person in the room. It is rare, for example, that students take notes on what other students say. In process groups, however, the teacher plays a supportive role—it is the children who do most of the talking and who are clearly the ones whose contributions are most important. The leader's role is not to instruct but rather to guide the process.

Children speak only for themselves. The pronoun "I" is emphasized over "we" or "you." The object is to help students to express themselves more honestly, to clarify their own beliefs, and to respond to one another sensitively.

The teacher's attention is focused primarily on the dynamics and process of the group. It is not so much what the children say as *how* they say it, and their relationship to one another, that draws the leader's attention. Who is getting along with whom? What coalitions have formed? What degree of cohesion has developed? What are the children avoiding dealing with? What is the meaning of any silence?

Advantages and Disadvantages of Process Groups

Process groups have a number of advantages over individual helping efforts. For example, a crisis in the community could reveal that a number of children have concerns about a similar issue (drugs, violence, disasters, and so on). In groups you can obviously reach more children and make more efficient use of your time. Additionally, group structures provide a support system for change, teach children skills for succeeding in social situations, facilitate an atmosphere of intimacy and trust, and most importantly, provide opportunities for constructive feedback from their peers. A number of teachers also report that introducing process group experiences into their classrooms also makes their jobs more fun. They feel as if they are truly making a difference in children's lives when they can observe *significant* changes in the way they think, feel, and behave in a relatively short period of time.

Process groups are not without their disadvantages, however. Because they can be such powerful educational and therapeutic modalities, they have the potential to do as much harm as good. Indeed, more than a few people have suffered emotional casualties in groups because the leader was untrained or unprepared to handle critical situations. Leading process groups thus requires more skills and a higher degree of leadership competence than do ordinary teaching responsibilities or even individual work with children. Peer pressure, forced conformity, less control, and increased complexity all contribute to a situation in which a teacher can quickly feel over his or her head if not adequately prepared.

These disadvantages and advantages are summarized below.

Table 5.1.   Advantages and Disadvantages of Group Work

Advantages	Disadvantages
Uses resources more efficiently	Confidentiality difficult to enforce
Encourages intimacy and trust	Requires more skill and competence
Provides support system for change	Forces conformity and peer pressure
Teaches skills for interpersonal success	Students receive less help and attention
Provides opportunities for vicarious learning	Leader has less control and influence
Helps kids practice new behaviors	Casualties can occur, especially when leaders are untrained and students are pressured to do
Provides honest feedback	things they don't feel ready for
Makes the teacher's job more fun	

If you wish to lead process group activities in your classes to facilitate children's emotional maturity, in addition to their academic achievement, you should keep several things in mind:

1. Don't attempt *any* structure without supervision available from someone who has more training (such as a school counselor, social worker, or psychologist).

2. Do not force children to disclose personal material beyond what they feel is comfortable. Casualties are most likely to occur when people do more than they are ready to do.

3. Since peer pressure is so strong among children, the individual rights of each participant need to be protected.

4. Understand clearly that there are specific times when you as a leader must intervene in order to protect the safety of the children and to ensure that your groups run smoothly.

When to Intervene in Groups

Research on effective group leadership has identified instances when you will need to do something specific to prevent people from getting hurt or to move the process along. We recommend that you memorize this list, or at least keep it close enough to refer to, until you log considerable experience as process leader. Intervention is called for under the following circumstances:

1. To stop abusive behavior or hostility. It is never permissible for group members to be disrespectful or abusive toward one another. Whenever you witness that one or more children are treating others in ways that may be hurtful, you must step in to help redirect the tone: "Candy, how might you tell Frank the same thing but this time in a way that will not hurt his feelings? Then perhaps you, Frank, could tell Candy how you are feeling right now."

2. To enforce rules that have been agreed on. The usual way of beginning any process group is to create and negotiate rules of conduct regarding what behavior is acceptable and what is not. Generally, some guidelines are developed regarding confidentiality, speaking only for yourself, being respectful and caring during interactions, to name but a few. The leader's role is not so much to enforce these rules as to ensure that group members comply with them: "I notice that Danny has come in late again. How do you guys want to handle this?"

3. *To cut off distractions and digressions.* Because group time is so valuable and there is so much to do, the leader serves an important function by keeping things on track and not permitting any single member to dominate or control discussions. Some students also need direct feedback regarding their interpersonal styles that may be irritating or counterproductive: "Fred, I notice that you were rolling your eyes skyward as Jon was talking. Perhaps you could be helpful to him and let him know how you react when he takes so long to get his points across."

4. *To model appropriate ways of being.* One of the most powerful roles that you can play as a teacher in general, and a group leader in particular, is to demonstrate the particular ways in which you want children to act. This modeling can take place in the ways you present yourself, the skills you demonstrate, the confidence and serenity you exude, or even the language you use to express yourself: "Notice that I just said that *I upset myself* over what just happened, meaning that nobody else did this to me; *I did it to myself* based on the way I interpreted the situation. When I speak like that I am reminding myself that, ultimately, I am in control of how I choose to feel."

5. *To spice up boredom or passivity.* Groups, like classrooms, can become predictable and stale without some intervention on the part of the leader to stir things up occasionally. There are no limits to the creative actions that you can take to breathe some life into a group—using humor, spontaneous actions, roleplaying, almost anything to get children's energy flowing: "OK, you guys are acting like you are asleep. Let's try something a little different. I want each one of you to pretend to be someone else in this group for the next 15 minutes but don't say who you are imitating. Let's see if any of us can recognize ourselves."

6. To correct irrational or distorted thinking. In one of the previous examples we mentioned that the language people used is symptomatic of what they are thinking inside. By changing the ways we talk to ourselves we also change our perceptions and subsequent actions based on these interpretations. It is thus common for group leaders to intervene when children speak in self-defeating or irrational ways:

Externalizing:	"How can I do better in school when everyone else is trying to sabotage me?"
Exaggerating:	"This is the worst day of my life; it is the worst day that I will ever have in my life."
Self-judging:	"I am the worst soccer player who ever lived. I'm so bad I'll never be good at anything."
Denying responsibility:	"It's not my fault. I just have bad luck."
Distorting:	"If I don't get what I want, I'll just die."

In each case, the group leader jumps in to correct the way the child is expressing him- or herself: "You mean that if you don't get what you want, you will be slightly disappointed."

7. To reinforce disclosures. Similar to classroom behavior modification, whenever a child does something that we want to continue, and want other children to imitate, we reinforce that behavior. "Tammy, I really like the way you just asserted yourself, and yet you did so in a very diplomatic and gentle way." We may also wish to systematically support behaviors such as disclosing, being direct and concise, cooperativeness, caring, and taking constructive risks.

8. To provide structure as needed. Groups flounder when they have either too much structure or not enough direction. Initially, when teachers make the transition from the classroom to process group settings, they tend to be too controlling in trying to ensure a successful experience. There are also times when groups meander because participants are not sure what is expected. Generally, it is better to provide more structure in the beginning stages of groups and then eventually allow children to assume more and more responsibility for where things go.

9. *To stop complaining.* Once children feel safe it does not take long for things to turn into a "gripe session." Kids will complain about other teachers, their parents, the weather, lost opportunities, any number of possibilities, and this litany of injustices is often not helpful. One rule we like is to talk only about things that we can do something about: "David, I appreciate the fact that it is hard for you with the reputation that you have created. We can't do anything about the past now, nor can we stop other people from saying what they like about you, but we sure can help you to act differently in the future. Let's concentrate on that instead."

10. *To comfort someone feeling anxious.* At times we sense the beginning signs that a child is really struggling with something. Tears are on the verge of flowing. We observe agitation or withdrawal or anger seething. Intervention is sometimes required to make sure that a child feels supported: "Donny, you look like you are having a really hard time right now. How can we help you?"

11. *To confront inconsistencies.* Direct confrontation is in order whenever someone is doing something that is self-defeating or self-contradicting. Whereas we might model these interventions initially, after a while children pick up the tune, and then they can do the work themselves, especially with cues from the leader: "Cassandra, you look puzzled by what Nathan is saying, as if something doesn't fit right wifh what he said earlier. Why don't you tell him what you heard?"

12. *To give constructive feedback.* Similar to modeling direct confrontation when indicated, we also want to demonstrate ways to give others the benefit of how we observe them. After we have given such feedback a few times, children pick up the

behavior and continue doing it for one another. Ideally, feedback is most constructive when it is specific, phrased sensitively, and comes with a supporting example: "Dana, one reason why you aren't taken very seriously is the way you express yourself. You don't make eye contact, you giggle a lot, and put yourself down as you speak. Can anyone else offer Dana some ideas about how she sabotages herself?"

Each of these group process interventions are added to the repertoire of skills we have already reviewed in previous chapters. It is just as appropriate for you to reflect feelings and content or to summarize what people say at various junctures, in groups as in individual sessions.

Varieties of Group Process

Teachers routinely incorporate group process activities into their curricula in a number of ways. They do so to spice up their classes, to supplement academic learning with emotional growth experiences, and to help children deal with the important issues they are struggling with—such as peer acceptance, personal identity, values clarification, moral and emotional development, relationship problems, stress management, and other adjustment difficulties that are part of daily life.

Teachers employ process structures because they recognize that a number of students are struggling with similar issues. One child approaches you because she is upset about a friend whose mother was killed in a car accident, but you have noticed that several others seem to have been profoundly affected. Some children seem more reticent than usual. Others have been acting out more than normal. Several parents have also reported that their children have expressed an unusual amount of worry about their safety. In such circumstances teachers sense that talking about the accident openly, especially in relation to children's fears, would be appropriate. This is just one example of how a process group experience might be used to help children clarify and express their feelings. Other examples of process groups follow.

Structured Group Activities

These kinds of exercises are quite familiar to teachers who want to help students personalize class material. They can be as simple as dividing a class into subgroups to discuss how they feel about a film they viewed, a book they read, or music they heard, or they can be as elaborate as a series of structured values clarification exercises that take place throughout a week, semester, or year. Usually, specific outcomes are desired, ones that help children achieve greater self-awareness and understanding of others.

Imagine, for example, that a social studies teacher is presenting a unit on discrimination. She might give her students a series of activities designed to help them become aware of their own prejudices and how such prejudices develop. An art teacher might show her students a painting and ask them to respond to it aesthetically.

The "tribes" model of cooperative learning is based on a set of structured group norms that emphasize sharing personal concerns and feelings, expressing positive regard for one another, and working as a team to complete assigned tasks. Rules are established for all interactions in which (1) confidentiality is enforced, (2) attentive listening to one another is required, (3) negative remarks are avoided, and (4) participants have the right to personal privacy. These group norms are intended to create a "tribal" community among students that makes it safe to explore new areas, express creativity, and develop intimacy without fear of criticism, rejection, or failure.

Consistent with process groups, responsibility is shifted from the teacher to the students to enforce the rules, draw one another out in discussion, and initiate interaction. The teacher's role is to facilitate the process by providing structure, exploring issues, asking questions, introducing activities, and assigning tasks as indicated. The goals are to encourage responsible and caring behavior.

Fishbowl Structures

The teacher works with a smaller group of children in the middle of the room with the rest of the class forming a circle around them. The observers may be assigned a "partner" inside the group to observe and give feedback to afterwards, or they may be given certain observational tasks regarding the group process itself.

The participants inside the "fishbowl" are afforded a more intimate experience in which they demonstrate principles that the observers can also learn vicariously. After a round of this, observers and participants switch roles.

A class of high school students was invited to explore gender differences in a dramatic way. The girls in the class were invited into the fishbowl and instructed to pretend that they were boys sitting around doing and talking about whatever they think boys do when they get together. Before too long, they were playing out exaggerated roles of boys talking about football and sex, acting like macho jocks, laughing uproariously throughout the discussion.

When the boys' turn came to act like a group of girls getting together, they too played their roles to the hilt, strutting and preening the way they imagined that feminine, helpless girls would act. Needless to say, the girls observing the scenario outside the fishbowl were no more amused than the boys were when they watched the girls mocking them.

A spirited discussion then ensued with the class at large, both boys and girls talking about how they felt trapped by their sex roles. They expressed their resentment at being ridiculed and resolved to be more sensitive to gender differences in the future.

Guidance Groups

If school counselors had the time, the resources, and the support staff, they would devote most of their time to guidance groups and hence reap the most benefits for children. Kids need help with many areas that are not part of the academic curriculum. In fact, if you asked children to make a list of the subjects that they would most like to study if they could create their own curriculum, we probably would not see English, mathematics, social studies, science, history, Spanish, and humanities on the tops of their lists—at least as they are conventionally taught. Instead, we might hear that they would prefer to learn about the opposite sex; relationships (what makes them work and what makes them fall apart); parents (how to get them to do your bidding); and other topics of timely interest.

Guidance groups are geared toward supplementing children's learning in academic subjects with specialized training in more pragmatic areas of immediate interest. This format is more familiar to you than many of the other kinds of groups because it offers primarily didactic instruction. Whether designed to address problem solving or study skills, career exploration, or communication skills, this group format allows you to present practical information about a subject of great interest to children and then help them to individualize what they learned to their own unique situations.

Support Groups

A group of teachers in one school district became alarmed by the number of children who reported violence in their neighborhoods. They observed how so many of the academic and discipline problems that they encountered seemed to be triggered by what the children were experiencing in their communities. With the counselors in their district overworked and understaffed, the teachers resolved to institute several measures to address the problem.

Support groups were organized in the schools under the guidance of a few counselors who recognized that teachers often had a much better handle on the daily lives of children. The teachers were prepared as teams of two co-leaders and assigned to begin support groups in their schools. In addition to the problem of violence, another major problem was identified in the area of drug/alcohol abuse (by children or their parents). Groups were thus targeted to these two different interest areas and followed a "curriculum" that consisted of providing opportunities for students to talk about their common concerns; to receive feedback from one another about what works and what doesn't; to learn they are not alone in their struggles, that others share their fears and apprehensions; and finally, to lend support to each other during these times of stress.

Getting Support for Yourself

The best way to learn to lead process groups is to recruit a partner who knows more than you do. With a more experienced co-leader you will appease many of your justifiable apprehensions about venturing into this unknown territory and also provide yourself a safety net when the going gets tough. A co-leader can model for you alternative ways to begin, maintain, and end group experiences. He or she can also give you valuable feedback after each session regarding aspects of your leadership style that you can work to improve.

Whether you find this partner among your own staff—a counselor, administrator, or another teacher—or whether you invite someone from the local university to supervise you in the field, a co-leader will give you the added boost of confidence and support necessary when undertaking an exciting yet frightening new adventure.

Suggested Activities

1. Observe the dynamics and processes that take place in the groups to which you currently belong—at school, work, home, and at play. What characteristic roles do you play in these groups? What are your strengths and weaknesses as a group member and potential leader? Note these reactions in a journal or share them aloud in a group discussion.

2. Select a structured group activity that accesses children's values, feelings, and beliefs—especially one that you would feel comfortable implementing. Try out this activity with a group of children, classmates, or friends. Solicit feedback from them afterward as to what they liked and disliked about the experience.

3. Identify someone who has experience leading groups and who may agree to work with you as a co-leader of a support group. Approach the person (a school counselor, school psychologist, school social worker, senior colleague with advanced training, a counselor educator

from the local university) with a plan for the kind of group you might like to run.

4. Meet in a group with your peers and share experiences you have had as members of process groups. What did you learn from these experiences? What specific things did the leader(s) do that you most and least appreciated?

Suggested Readings

Corey, G., & Corey, M. S. (1991). *Groups: Process and practice* (4th ed.). Pacific Grove, CA: Brooks/Cole.

Drew, N. (1987). *Learning the skills of peacemaking: An activity guide for elementary-age children in communication, cooperation, resolving conflict.* Rolling Hills Estates, CA: Jalmar Press.

Gazda, G. M. (1989). *Group counseling: A developmental approach* (4th ed.). Boston: Allyn & Bacon.

Gibbs, J. (1987). *Tribes: A process for social development and cooperative learning.* Santa Rosa, CA: Center Source Publications.

Kreidler, W. M. (1984). *Creative conflict resolution: More than 200 activities for keeping peace in the classroom.* Glenview, IL: Scott, Foresman.

Krieg, F. J. (1988). *Group leadership training and supervision manual for adolescent group counseling in the schools* (3rd ed.) Muncie, IN: Accelerated Development.

Rohnke, K. (1984). *Silverbullets: A guide to initiating problems, adventure games and trust activities.* Dubuque, IA: Kendall/Hunt.

Being Skillful
in Parent Conferences

One of the most frustrating aspects of a teaching job is recognizing that in spite of all your best efforts and devotion to children's learning and welfare, there is actually little you can do without the cooperation of parents. Children are in your charge long enough for you to influence them in significant ways. Unfortunately, once they leave school, they may be in a distinctly different environment and culture that works at counter purposes to what has been accomplished in school.

Jonas is among your most talented protégés—the best and the brightest. There is no doubt that college is in his future, and after that, who knows? He is smart enough and personable enough to do anything he sets his mind to do.

Away from school, however, there are quite different forces at work. Jonas lives in a house with his mother, a half-dozen other children who are related to him in some way, and his mother's current lover. He is teased mercilessly by his half-siblings when he brings a book home. If he wants to read or study, there is no way he could do it with the chaos in his house—television blaring, kids fighting, mother and lover arguing, people coming and going. Jonas spends as little time at home as possible.

Jonas's mother knows her son is bright and has potential. She is doing the best she can to raise her children, mostly by herself. How dare those teachers insinuate she doesn't care about her son—or any of her children for that matter. What is this notice about another one of those teacher conferences? She'll show those know-it-all teachers this time. No way will she sit and listen to another lecture on "reading at home" or "sending her son to a special summer camp program." Maybe she'll just move to some other place where people will get off her back. Be the best thing for Jonas anyway.

When the Child Saves the Parents

Without parent cooperation teachers can do little to help enrich children's lives. One of the most important tasks a teacher can accomplish is to recruit parents as partners in the educational process. Yes, developing trusting relationships with children is the *main* part of our job, but unless we can do the same with their parents, our educational and helping efforts will be limited.

One of the more interesting areas of psychological research in the past few decades has been family systems—that is, recognizing the powerful forces at work in the relationships between parents and children. We now know that it is senseless to try and understand the actions of an individual child without examining the family context in which they take place. There are coalitions in families, hidden sources of power, and subtle lines of communication that motivate and inadvertently reinforce behavior behind the scenes.

Larry had previously been a very cooperative young man in school but recently he had developed a number of irritating mannerisms that invariably got under his teacher's skin. He was sent to the counselor for help and then later referred to a therapist in the community because of the apparent severity of his problems. The therapist saw the child for only a few sessions before there was remarkable improvement and Larry became his old self once again.

A few weeks later the therapist was again contacted by the school system, but this time it was about Larry's younger brother, Stephen, who had been caught setting off the school's fire alarm. This was especially puzzling because prior to this incident Stephen had been a model student—straight As and a leader in his class. Again, in a remarkably brief period of time, Stephen responded to counseling and resolved to stay out of trouble in the future. A few weeks later, the therapist was again contacted, but this time by the parents directly who were having trouble with their youngest son who was acting surly and belligerent around the house. "What has gotten into our children?" the parents asked. "They never had these problems before."

What indeed? Eventually it was learned that the parents were having marital problems that had escalated to the point where open warfare was taking place in the house. Screams of outrage and slammed doors punctuated the household on a regular basis as the two parents continuously badgered one another and threatened to walk out. About the only time they seemed to get along was when one of their children was in trouble. In such instances, they would temporarily call a truce and pool their efforts out of concern for their children. In one dramatic example of this phenomenon, the parents were arguing at the dinner table over which one was really at fault for their collective misery. Just before the argument escalated into a major conflict, Larry tossed a roll across the table at one of his younger brothers. Soon all three of them were involved in the skirmish, requiring the parents to stop arguing in order to put down the disturbance.

This pattern of a child acting out in order to distract the parents from their own troubles is not unusual. Although not usually a conscious action, the effects are nevertheless quite powerful: As long as the child is having problems in school, the parents join forces in order to be of assistance; once the child straightens out, the parental conflicts or other family skirmishes resume. The child's acting out behavior thus serves a stabilizing function within the family.

The implications of these family dynamics are profound for teachers who wish to understand why certain children are troubled and why they, inexplicably, are acting out with no apparent gain. This example can also help you understand the crucial nature of parent-teacher communication: Unless you can coordinate what you are doing with the people with whom the children live, your best efforts will fall short. Thus, as dreaded as they may be for some teachers, parent conferences represent your best opportunity to gather important information about your children's family situations and, sometimes, to even have constructive influence on parents' behavior so that they may more effectively support what you are doing— and vice versa.

The Functions of Parent-Teacher Conferences

Sitting on the top of the memos and announcements in the Spanish teacher's school mailbox was a parent conference request form from Susie's mother. Susie, a ninth-grade student, was a quiet girl who kept pretty much to herself. Although she was a cheerleader, she did not really mingle with the other students. She was dependable, always had her books and a pencil in class, and received average grades. With a soft voice, Susie responded when called on, participated in activities, and never talked out of turn. Any teacher would have been happy to have her in class. Her Spanish teacher could only wonder at the purpose of this conference.

She began to get organized for the meeting during her preparation period. First, she pulled out a copy of her course description, which included class expectations and grading procedures. Then, she made a list of all the assignments, quizzes, and tests she had given along with Susie's grades. Next, she gathered examples of Susie's work to show her mother, followed by a collection of the forthcoming assignments. Finally, the teacher looked at the list of parents who had signed in at Open House to see if Susie's mother had attended and checked her telephone file cards to see if she had ever talked to her before for any reason. She had learned long ago that preparation was extremely important before meeting with any parent.

After school, the teacher rearranged the furniture in the room, placing two student desks together so they would face one another. She organized all the materials and then sat anxiously wondering what was on Mrs. Tanner's mind. She found out soon enough. During the course of the conference she learned that it had been Susie's decision to take Spanish despite her mother and counselor's preference that she wait until tenth grade. In addition, Mrs. Tanner revealed that her daughter was a competitive swimmer with a state ranking who would miss many days of school while participating in meets. She was concerned about Susie's grades. The teacher continued to listen and encouraged the parent to talk: She learned that Susie was indeed very shy in certain situations even though she was a cheerleader. Mrs. Tanner's conference provided her with additional insight and background information into her student's behavior. She developed an appreciation of Susie's goals and determination to reach those goals. She was in a better position to help Susie in the future. This involved meeting with her individually to review and practice material presented in class, to schedule make-up assignments, and to make sure she was comfortable in class before including her in discussions.

Frequently, the thought of a parent-teacher conference puts the teacher on the defensive. Questions like "What does this parent want from me?" and "Who does this parent think he is?" come to mind. And, we ready a list of retorts such as: "I do *not* give too many homework assignments." "My tests are *not* too hard." "I do *not* pick on your son." Yet, more often than not, conferences are helpful and motivating. Parents want their children to do well. They want teachers to help their children. The information they give provides you with important insights that allow you to plan accordingly. The teacher in the previous example learned topics she could use to draw Susie into class participation. Furthermore, a team effort can help ensure a student stays on the path to success.

Mrs. Robert came to see her son's fourth-grade teacher after an Unsatisfactory Progress Report had been sent home. Rudy was failing, and his behavior in school was erratic. Mrs. Robert told the teacher at the beginning of the conference that if her son misbehaved, to go ahead and beat him because that's what she did at home. The teacher suggested that perhaps they might talk about other alternatives, because physical punishment is often not very effective, and even when it does work, there are certain negative side effects. But first, she reviewed with Mrs. Robert what the expectations were for school and what materials Rudy was to bring each day.

Once a collaborative relationship was established, Mrs. Robert was more than willing to explore ways that she might help. In the course of the conversation Mrs. Robert told the teacher that Rudy was the youngest in the family. (Did being "babied" contribute to his immature behavior, the teacher wondered.) Her two older sons were attending college. Rudy's ambition was to be a singer. Even in fourth-grade he had been selected for the boy's choir, a rare honor. Now, *there* was a talent the teacher could put to use. She made a note to involve singing in her lesson plans the next day. Maybe she could challenge Rudy to learn through music and channel some of his energy.

In both examples, the functions of parent-teacher conferences are highlighted: (1) to gather helpful information about the child's interests and abilities; (2) to observe the family dynamics in action and note clues that might explain a child's behavior; (3) to recruit the parents' assistance as partners in the educational process; and (4) to work in concert with parents to achieve mutually agreed on goals.

Directing a Constructive Conference

In many ways, a parent-teacher conference is like an improvisational play: There is a general script to follow but with lots of room for spontaneous action. You are the director as well as one of the main characters. The parents and child form the rest of the cast, although they may be unclear about their roles. Each of you is probably rehearsing a part in anticipation of what the other might say or do. Careful thought will need to be given to every facet of the production in order for the performance to go smoothly.

Setting the Stage. Just as there are different kinds of plays— dramas, musicals, comedies—so is there an assortment of parent-teacher conferences, each with its own unique plot development and script structure. Essentially, conferences come about in three ways: (1) initiated by the parent (if there is a perceived problem); (2) initiated by the teacher (if a consultation may help to gather information or solicit assistance); and (3) initiated by the system (regularly scheduled meetings each semester). Depending on who initiates the meeting, your goals will be somewhat different. In the case of conferences requested by parents you will rely primarily on listening skills. Those scheduled by you will involve more questioning and information gathering on your part, as well as problem solving. The kind that involve routine reports on progress will be the most structured of all, and in these you will lead a focused discussion and work on establishing a good alliance with the parents.

In setting the stage for each of these conferences you will consider a number of questions: When and where will the conference be held? Allow plenty of time. Don't schedule appointments too close together if it can be avoided.

Who will be participating? Will an interpreter be needed? Some teachers like to include the student in the process. Rather than being a "subject on trial," the student can be an active participant in the planning process, often giving valuable input and insight. "What are some things you would like to accomplish in this meeting with your parents?" "What role would you like me to play as a mediator?" "How will you react when I bring up those disturbances that occurred in class?" The student is not only warned about what will occur but can come to view the meeting with shared responsibility for its successful outcome. Some teachers are instituting student-led conferences wherein the student takes responsibility for all stages, from planning to chairing the conference, developing leadership skills along the way. The student enjoys the attention received from parent(s) and teacher in this positive, constructive environment. The teacher works with the student in developing the communication skills needed and collecting a portfolio of student work to present at the conference. The teacher finds the amount of work she has to do in preparation for the conference is lessened and her role in the conference shifts from leader to resource person.

At times it's inappropriate to include the student, such as when there is a serious problem in the home, or when control issues are dominant. Remember that each additional person adds another dimension to the relationships operating at the conference.

In staging the setting for the conference consider where the furniture is placed—sitting behind a desk can create a symbolic barrier. A face-to-face position will lend itself to a more cooperative and sharing atmosphere. You will need comfortable seats for all the people attending the conference. The location of the meeting also needs to be considered; try to find a place with the least amount of distractions. (You can always post a note on the door asking not to be disturbed.)

As far as props, you will want a folder of the student's work, his or her grades, and assignments. You might also prepare a list of questions you have about the student and a loose script of what you hope to accomplish.

The Introduction. If this is the first conference with the parent, greet the parent at the office and introduce yourself to him or her. Shake hands and make eye contact. As you guide the parent to the meeting room, begin conversation with a positive comment about the student. "He always says hello to me in the morning." "She does her homework very neatly." "Billy told me he just got his Water Safety Instruction card. You must be very proud of him." Give parents a moment to look around the room and get their bearings.

Interaction Begins. A good place to begin is by asking a general open-ended question about the child. "What has Judy said about school at home?" Use your listening and exploration skills to seek information about the student that only a parent could provide. Review the purpose of the conference. If the student is present, give him or her an opportunity to talk, ask questions, and state his or her feelings. Close this stage of the conference by summarizing consensual goals you have agreed on.

Problem Solving. Describe the student's behavior and school work, pointing out his or her strengths and weaknesses. Identify objectives for the semester. Ask the student to describe his or her own perception of the problem. What obstacles does he see? Differences of opinion can be acknowledged without being resolved; emphasize the points in common. Focus on possible strategies that will help the student. What needs to be done? Who can help? When? Where? How often? Develop a schedule, a timeline. Determine the parent's responsibility and the child's responsibility, as well as your own role in reaching desired goals.

Evaluation. Consider how progress will be determined. How will follow-up plans be made to evaluate the results? Make plans for future communication between the parent and teacher. Will you schedule another conference, talk by telephone, or send home a progress report?

Conclusion. Invite each participant to summarize what they understand from the conference and what they intend to do. You may wish to write down a list of points or have the student take notes. Thank the parent for sharing information with you and for planning for the child's success in school. Ask for feedback on what you can do to be most helpful in the future.

The Reviews. After the conference has been completed, spend some time reflecting on your performance and noting areas for improvement.

Did you help the parent feel comfortable?

Were you able to answer the parent's questions?

Did you give the parent time to speak or did you do most of the talking?

Did you emphasize the student's strengths as well as his or her weaknesses?

Did you keep the conference focused on the student and not the parent or the school?

Was a plan developed? Were important points summarized?

Does each person know his or her responsibility?

Was there anything you forgot to mention that you would like to include next time?

When the Play Doesn't Go as Planned

Even the most experienced teachers have difficulties at times. Parents are not always as cooperative and pleasant as we would like them to be. Single parents and working parents, for example, find it difficult to schedule appointments. If a parent brings his or her own personal problems to the conference, they might take priority over the problems of the child. The parent may need a sounding board before he or she can look at the problems of the child. Sometimes, interactions become heated and tempers flare. There may also be some resentment toward the teacher as an authority figure or a representative of an institution viewed as repressive or uncaring. For these and other reasons you will encounter parents who appear less interested in helping their child than they do in knocking you for a loop.

You may find yourself dealing with difficult parents who are either frightened and defensive or extremely aggressive and demanding. We will review examples and discuss strategies for working with such challenging parents.

The Angry Parent

"My daughter does not cheat, and I resent you implying such a filthy lie!" Larisa had attempted to take a vocabulary test with the help of a "cheat sheet."

The teacher must recognize that anger is often due to frustration. The best approach in this situation is to let the parent vent his or her feelings while maintaining an accepting attitude. This will be very hard to do because you will also be feeling angry for having your integrity questioned. Self-control, however, will serve you well. Use your reflection and listening skills until the anger loses its momentum. Don't argue or you will only aggravate matters further.

Change the focus of the discussion to one of problem solving in which you attempt to enlist the parent's help in resolving the difficulties. A general rule to keep in mind during any interpersonal struggle is this: When you are doing something that doesn't work, don't do it anymore; try something else. If trying to change the parent's mind isn't successful, rather than redoubling your efforts, try backing off instead. Try anything other than what isn't working. But do not, under any circumstances, let things escalate into a shouting match. Inner tranquility can best be maintained if you talk to yourself throughout the encounter, reminding yourself that this isn't personal, that the parent is just doing the best he or she can, and that nothing will be gained by trying to humiliate him or her.

Naturally, you must draw the line if the parent becomes disrespectful or abusive. At that point suggest that a colleague or administrator join you as mediator. Rescheduling an appointment at another time is also effective because the parent will have had time to regain composure.

We give you fair warning that no matter how conciliatory, easy going, and nonconfrontational you may be, there will definitely come a time when a parent will jump all over you for no legitimate reason that you can identify. Try to prepare yourself for such an encounter in advance so that you are not so surprised that you cannot gather your wits about you and act professionally.

The Disappointed Parent

"I don't know what I can do," said Mrs. Cohen. She was disappointed that her son had received a D on his report card. "He's such a good boy. We had such high hopes for him, but he just doesn't seem to care about school."

Parents can sabotage their children just as much by being overinvolved as by being neglectful. Some children feel a tremendous sense of power in being able to say to their parents, "You can't make me do anything that I don't want to do. And just to prove it, I will do the opposite of what you want."

Some parents also have unrealistic expectations for their children. Regardless of the child's interests or talents, the parents press him or her to live out their own aspirations. This is also likely to result in disappointment.

Disappointed parents need someone who will hear them out. You can be of invaluable assistance by helping them to do a "reality check," comparing what they expect versus what is possible. You can also help them to understand the degree to which they are imposing their own goals on their children, who may have agendas of their own. Finally, you can help them to sort out what they may be doing to contribute to the disappointing results. Applying the strategy we mentioned in the previous section, a parent was helped to realize that nagging his child to do homework not only decreased the likelihood that it would be completed but actually guaranteed that the child would rebel. By backing off a bit the child was given the freedom to assume more responsibility for his own life rather than feeling like he was always disappointing his father.

The Troubled Parent

"Jenny is just getting to be too much for me to handle. With all the things that have happened to me lately I just can't seem to concentrate very well. I know Jenny needs my help, but sometimes I just can't find the energy."

The troubled parent needs someone outside his or her circle of family and friends to listen. In some situations you will be viewed as a professional who is both compassionate and highly skilled—and you can do a lot for someone who is troubled by helping them feel understood. In most circumstances, however, your main task is to develop a trusting enough relationship with the troubled parent so that she will respect your advice to get help from a professional. Depressed, anxious, or otherwise suffering parents are in no position to help their children. Your job is to urge them to consult a professional therapist or physician, if not for their own good, then certainly for the benefit of children who are being shortchanged.

The task of encouraging someone to seek professional help is not as easy as it sounds: People who are experiencing emotional difficulties are often resistant to the idea of seeing a mental health professional because of fears that they will be labeled as "crazy." You can pave the way for parents by addressing their concerns and then firmly encouraging them to follow through with their resolve.

The Manipulative Parent

"I know you said on the phone that you wouldn't change my daughter's grade, and I certainly respect your professional judgment in these matters, but . . . ."

Not all parents you meet will be straightforward as to what they want from you; some will have hidden agendas that involve getting you to do things that you don't want to do, or feel uncomfortable doing. The issue of changing grades is just one such example. Others may include the parent who wants you to give special preference to his or her child. Another may want you to make unreasonable arrangements or to accommodate inappropriate requests.

The intrinsic conflict of these situations is that some parents want something from you. They know that if the request is put to you directly, you will say no. So they resort to manipulative, devious, underhanded ways to get their way. Some of these parents will attempt to intimidate you by exploiting their power ("I have a good friend on the School Board") or by threatening you ("I just may have to initiate disciplinary action against you if you persist in being so close-minded about this").

There are no easy answers for dealing with manipulative parents. We mention this circumstance more as a warning to you than as a situation that has definite solutions. We simply urge you to stand by your professional standards and not give in to manipulative ploys. But you must recognize what is happening before it is too late. Such awareness comes from experience.

Good supervision and support also are crucial, especially to you in the early part of your career—not only in learning the ins and outs of conducting parent conferences but in all facets of your work. When you encounter manipulative parents you will need someone in your corner— your principal, a mentor, a senior colleague, someone who can lend support and advise you how to make it through the traps that have been set.

The Quiet Parent

This individual can be one of the most challenging parents to make contact with in a conference. Because of nervousness, uncertainty about what is expected, or just a passive personality, some parents will sit throughout the conference and barely say a word. You may find yourself babbling to fill the time and then feel very uncomfortable about what took place.

What to do with a quiet parent depends very much on why the person is reticent. Your first assignment, therefore, should be to try and make such a determination: "I notice that you are not saying very much." The parent will then clarify that he feels a little uncomfortable, or that he doesn't know what you expect, or that he just doesn't talk much. (You can verify the last assumption if he replies to your statement by saying, "Yup.")

In most cases, be patient so that the parent will come to know and trust you enough to open up a bit. Remember, however, that if you attempt to fill the silences with a nonstop monologue, then the parent will never have the chance to engage with you. Every conference has its own pace and distinct characteristics. If you remain sensitive and responsive to each parent's personality, then you can adapt your style of interaction to fit the unique requirements of the situation. In some conferences, the parent will do most of the talking; in others, you will take more of a direct lead. The more flexible you can be in the way you conduct conferences, the more likely that you will develop positive working relationships with a variety of parents from diverse cultures, backgrounds, and personal situations.

We do not wish to make you unduly apprehensive or mistrustful about the parents you will encounter—the vast majority will be cooperative, respectful, and very grateful for your high degree of dedication and competence. Be warned, however, that at least once a semester you will probably meet at least one parent who will not be very pleasant for you to work with.

Multicultural Perspectives

Flexibility is indeed the key to building trust and respect in your relationships with parents. It requires knowledge of the diverse cultural backgrounds from which your children originate and a willingness on your part to do what it takes to help individuals with different values, needs, and interests feel comfortable. You have already learned the importance of multicultural sensitivity with respect to reaching children; the same principles apply to working with their parents.

You will need to learn about the attitudes and customs of the cultures from which your students come in order to (1) understand the behavior patterns of the children and their parents and (2) avoid problems of miscommunication. In particular, pay attention to nonverbal communication. For example, in many ethnic groups it is considered rude to look at an adult "in the eye." For this reason people look down rather than at a speaker. Different attitudes toward competition explain why some students will turn to others for help during a test. Cooperation rather than competition may be emphasized at home. Certain cultures frown on women in authoritative roles. Consequently, a female teacher may have difficulty establishing rapport with male parents without knowing why. Developing an appreciation and awareness of the various groups from which your students come will facilitate your interactions with them.

Suggested Activities

1. Explore the dynamics of your family history, noting the impact of your parents' conduct on your own behavior at school. Try to recall a specific instance in which something your parents did or said had a dramatic impact on your life. What could a teacher have done to intervene with your parents on your behalf?

2. Recruit a few friends or colleagues to help you role-play a parent conference. Concentrate on applying the helping skills (especially questioning and active listening) during your interaction.

3. With your partners, you take on the role of an angry or defensive parent who feels threatened by the teacher's influence and authority over his or her child. After the interaction, talk about your feelings and reactions *from the parent's point of view.* What did it feel like to have your competence as a parent challenged?

4. Write a sample letter to parents describing the objectives of a parent-teacher conference. Include what you hope to accomplish, what the parents might expect to occur, where and when the meeting will take place, and what can be done in preparation.

5. Interview a sample of parents who have children of different ages. Ask them what their best and worst experiences have been in conferences with teachers. Solicit their advice about some things that you might do differently.

6. Interview several teachers to ask about their favorite methods of leading parent conferences. Ask how they prepare for the meetings, how they keep themselves in control when they are being challenged, how they keep parents focused on the goals of the meeting, and how they use the time most effectively.

Suggested Readings

Kottler, J. A. (1992). *Compassionate therapy: Working with difficult clients.* San Francisco: Jossey-Bass.

Little, A. W., & Allan, J. (1989). Student-led parent-teacher conferences. *Elementary School Guidance and Counseling, 23,* 210-218.

Rich, D. (1987). *Teachers and parents: An adult-to-adult approach.* Washington, DC: National Education Association.

Rotter, J. D., Robinson, E. H., & Fey, M. A. (1987). *Parent-teacher conferencing.* Washington, DC: National Education Association.

Simpson, R. L. (1990). *Conferencing parents of exceptional children* (2nd ed.). Austin, TX: Pro-Ed.

Consulting Effectively
With Other Professionals

No matter how knowledgeable and skilled you are in the counseling process, no matter how comfortable and adept you become in the various roles you play, no matter how proficiently you are able to communicate with others, assess children's problems, understand their underlying issues, and design effective helping strategies—you will still need the assistance of a number of other professionals and specialists in your work. The best teachers functioning in counseling roles are, in fact, those who can diagnose accurately that a problem exists and know where and to whom to turn for expert guidance.

Teachers not only serve as consultants to others, such as parents and children, but they often solicit the services of experts when they require specialized help. You will ask for outside assistance for several reasons:

- To gain the benefit of expertise that is outside your specialty
- To help you look at fresh or innovative solutions to problems that you face

- To get a more detached and objective perspective on what you are experiencing
- To get help handling tasks that you do not have the time or inclination to complete
- To provide you with training in a particular area of need

Consulting With Other Teachers

"Boogie," said the 6'2" football player after the teacher called the name Thomas Barlett III on the first day of school.

"Boogie?" she questioned. She had asked the students to tell her what name they preferred to be called.

"Boogie," he affirmed.

This was a nickname the teacher was not too sure about. So she went to one of the coaches after school who explained that everyone called the young man Boogie and that there was no need for concern.

Once you walk into a school building you will find that you are not alone. You will be surrounded by people who will likely go out of their way to help you—your fellow teachers. Immediately you will have the opportunity to network with people teaching the same grade or subject area as you are. In a large school the head of the department will serve as a resource person for you. Many schools establish a Buddy System where you will be assigned a teacher who has agreed to serve as your Big Brother or Big Sister and guide you through the maze of school routines, rituals, and papers to be filled out. Certain teachers will reach out to you. They will help you put "crises" in perspective, show you the "tricks of the trade," give you background on students if you want it, and explain school traditions. At the same time, you will have to figure out where you belong. Cliques form in every social situation, some with higher walls than others. In one school, the majority of teachers ate lunch in the faculty dining room. A small group of male teachers played cards while they ate lunch in the faculty lounge. One teacher didn't want to eat lunch with either group, so he sat in the cafeteria and ate with the students. As you develop relationships with the people on the staff of the school, including custodians, librarians, hall monitors, and secretaries, you will find many people to turn to and people who will turn to you.

Mindy had developed a negative attitude in her geography class after neglecting to study for a test and failing it. Her choir was going on a two-day trip to perform in a competition, and her teacher was concerned that Mindy would get behind in her classwork and that her attitude would further deteriorate. When Mindy asked her teacher to sign a release from class, the teacher deferred doing so for a day in order to speak to the choir director about the situation. The two teachers decided to talk to Mindy together regarding her behavior and grades in geography. Mindy admitted she hadn't studied and promised to make time for homework. She also agreed to complete the assignments she would be missing ahead of the field trip so that when she returned she would be at the same point as the rest of the class.

Many schools have a policy that a student's participation in extracurricular activities depends on his or her maintaining certain grades or grade point average. So, if a student's behavior or grades are becoming questionable, speak to the band director, club sponsor, coach, or whoever sponsors the activity to see if you can work together to help the student.

Your fellow teachers have a wealth of experience from which to draw. Whether you have questions of discipline, implementation of the curriculum, ordering supplies, or if you just need to talk about a "bad day," these people can be a support system for you.

Consulting With the Principal

Administrators can also be a tremendous source of inspiration, support, and guidance. They are mentors in the truest sense of having someone in your corner whose main function is to make your job easier.

Perhaps one of your greatest challenges is to develop a working relationship with the administrator who evaluates your work. Relationships such as this are not built overnight; trust builds slowly. Of course, you can help the process along—and not just wait for the other person to make the overtures. Invite the principal to stop by your room to see projects that the students have created or a bulletin board you put up as a teaching aid. Invite him or her to participate in a class activity. This tactic offers the principal an opportunity to get involved in your domain, and it also lets him or her know what is going on in your classroom. Speak to the principal on a positive note, giving feedback, for example, on an assembly that went smoothly, or an extracurricular activity, or a staff development session that you found particularly meaningful. Report on progress of committee work. Approach him or her with your ideas or suggestions for improvements.

School administrators are expert problem solvers. Let them know when you need assistance. Remember, they were in your shoes once. They are familiar with the frustrations of teaching, although they may need to be reminded of the specific difficulties you experience in your field. Whether your school becomes the best place you have ever worked or a land mine of potential obstacles and dangers depends to a large part on the relationships you forge with administrators and department heads. Whether in industry or education, developing a relationship with a supervisor, who could potentially become a caring mentor, is crucial for job satisfaction and success within the system.

Consulting With Counselors

It was hard for Mr. Blane to describe the changes he had noticed in Teresa. She was maybe a little quieter, a bit more pensive than usual. She still did her work and participated in class discussions, but something was different about her energy level. He could not quite put his finger on it. Mr. Blane's attempts to communicate with her were quickly cut off. "How's it going?" was answered with the typical, "Fine." "How are you today?" "Good." End of conversation. He decided to visit the girl's counselor and ask her if she would discretely talk to the girl.

A few days later the counselor reported that there were indeed some problems in the family, things that Teresa preferred remained confidential. The counselor expressed gratitude for Mr. Blane's perceptive observations and reassured him that everything was once again under control. Mr. Blane was still intensely curious about what had happened with Teresa and her family, but the counselor explained that sometimes children prefer to talk to someone other than their teacher. In this case, because Teresa liked Mr. Blane so much, she did not want him to know anything about her that did not show her in the best light. Sometimes it happens that although we want to be helpful to students, our authority role prevents us from developing the kind of relationship that counselors are perfectly positioned and trained to create.

Whenever you can't seem to establish rapport with a particular student or the situation is too much for you to handle, counselors can provide the support and guidance you need. What will you do when you suspect a child is being abused or neglected? What about when a child approaches you for advice about using birth control? How will you handle the situation when you notice an abrupt change in a child's personality? Counselors can provide support, feedback, problem-solving skills. They can help you address issues of self-esteem and career education, or they can work directly with your students. They can teach communication skills, decision-making skills, developing self-control, cooperation skills, emotional control, and the ability to laugh at oneself rather than take oneself too seriously. They can lead self-help groups (with you as a co-leader, if you like). Furthermore, they can provide you and your students with resources in the community.

Sometimes you may consult with a counselor informally, such as in the case of Mr. Blane. Other times it may be best to handle the situation yourself with the guidance of the counselor. In either instance, counselors can be your best resources in addressing the emotional needs of your students, and of yourself.

Seeing a Counselor as Your Personal Consultant

A unique feature of counseling as a profession is that a person does not need to have an emotional disorder or even a "problem" to seek help. Whereas other mental health professionals such as psychiatrists, psychologists, and social workers specialize in treating severe mental disorders, counselors are experts in helping people with normal concerns of daily living. This includes, but is not limited to, adjustment problems or transitions to life changes, career development, finding meaning in one's life, developing better self-understanding, resolving relationship difficulties, planning for the future, reducing stress, and any other struggle that human beings face as a part of daily existence.

Although teaching is a very rewarding profession, it is also a stressful one—filled with demands, responsibilities, and commitments that sometimes seem beyond what any person could reasonably be expected to handle. As an authority figure, you will be a target for some children who wish to act out their frustration and hostility. Sometimes you will be caught in a tug of war between administrators, parents, and children, with no apparent escape in sight. Furthermore, the burnout rate in teaching is high because of what is expected from you.

Deciding to seek the services of a counselor (perhaps being referred by the counselor in your school) as your personal consultant can therefore help you in a number of ways:

1. An experience as a client can help you improve your own helping skills. By watching a professional at work, by noting what works best with you, you will find yourself unconsciously and deliberately adopting strategies to your own situations.
2. You will have a safe, confidential support system that will give you the opportunity to work through stresses and concerns without having to burden your family and friends.
3. You can motivate yourself to grow and to continue learning about those aspects of your functioning you wish to improve.
4. You can work through particular difficulties that crop up in your life. Issues that teachers are especially vulnerable to include a fear of failure, feelings of uncertainty as to whether the rewards of the profession are

worth the aggravation, feelings of stagnation, and conflicts with colleagues or administrators.

5. You can counteract the deleterious effects of classroom
life. On a regular basis you will be dealing with children
who do not necessarily want to be within your control
or domain; some will fight you every inch of the way.
The wear and tear takes its toll until, eventually, you will
start to feel serious effects—unless, of course, you have
developed coping skills to help you stay energized.

Many of these reasons for consulting a counselor are evident
in the testimony of one beginning teacher who did quite well
in her teacher education program, yet encountered a number of
adjustment difficulties her first year on the job:

"I really had no idea how hard it would be for me to finish
this first school year. Several times I wanted to quit. In fact,
I probably would have quit if I hadn't seen a counselor
during some difficult times.

"I was always so organized at the university. I kept up with
my assignments, did what I was told, got good grades. I
learned a lot. But I still wasn't adequately prepared for the
chaos I would have to deal with— a principal who had a style
that was somewhat less than supportive, colleagues who
were bickering, kids who showed no interest, parents who
cared even less. I was totally demoralized and started to
consider other career options.

"At the suggestion of a friend, I started seeing a counselor
recommended to me by one of our school counselors. At first,
I didn't much like it at all. I kept it a secret because I thought
people might think I was going crazy—actually, that is how
it felt to me.

"But then it started to feel so good to have somebody I
could talk to, someone who didn't judge me or tell me what
to do, someone who believed in me, who encouraged me
to look at some difficult aspects of myself that I don't much
like. I examined the very reasons why I wanted to be a
teacher in the first place. I even began to realize that it
wasn't just the kids and the parents and the administrators—it was me, too. There were some things that I had

been doing to make life more difficult than it needed to be. Wow! It was an amazing experience."

Consulting With the School Psychologist

Traditionally, school psychologists have focused most of their attention on testing and assessment of children for placement in special programs. However, as they add consulting to their repertoire of services, they offer a wealth of support and information in many areas from individual differences in learning styles and classroom dynamics to multicultural needs and effective behavior management strategies. They offer not only expertise in problem solving with individual students, but also prevention services for all students. They can offer programs on a variety of topics such as peer pressure, test anxiety, self-esteem, and loneliness. Furthermore, they will help you identify students "at risk" and develop programs for them.

When you experience a problem, you will probably feel considerable relief to know that you don't have to "go it alone." In some schools, your first step will be to present the problem for review to an in-school team consisting of several professionals. Then, if the need still persists, the screening committee will make a formal referral to the school psychologist. In other schools, the school psychologist is available to work with teachers directly. Both situations allow you to access the expertise of a professional trained specifically to assess children's difficulties and to prescribe programs for remediation.

Consulting With Faculty at the Local University

Education professors, instructors, and supervisors are often quite eager to provide help to teachers who are experiencing difficulties or who simply have questions on how to handle matters. The local university will also serve as a resource for you. You can invite college faculty (with the permission of your principal) to demonstrate the latest educational techniques in your classroom and/or meet with them to critique your teaching style. They are available to do workshops for you and your staff on particular areas of interest and many would be happy to consult with you regarding methods, materials, behavior management, and other concerns you might have.

One group of teachers in an elementary school was concerned about the high rate of single-parent homes in which their children resided. Because counselors in the district were at a premium, there were very little, if any, services offered to address this growing problem. The teachers approached their principal to see if she would support their intent to begin support groups for children experiencing problems adjusting to the separation of their parents. Together they decided to recruit the assistance of faculty at the university who trained them in the skills and methods of developing such a program. Once the groups began, the counselor education faculty remained available to provide ongoing supervision.

The Teacher's Role in Individualized Education Programs

The teacher is an active participant in the development of the Individualized Education Program (IEP) for a special education student. Having already consulted with the school psychologist, the teacher will also confer with the child's parent(s). Often it is the teacher who becomes aware that a problem exists. It is the teacher who usually first contacts the parent(s). It is the teacher who arranges for testing. As an advocate for the student, the teacher finds himself or herself as a central figure in working with the resource teachers, school psychologists, and parents as coordinator and disseminator of information. The teacher may be the only person present at the conference who knows everybody.

In particular, the teacher must be sensitive to the emotions and concerns of the parent(s). When parents are informed that a child may qualify for special help, they typically experience a pattern of reactions: shock, denial, guilt, anger, frustration. Of the people participating in an initial IEP, the teacher may be the

only person with whom the parents have had contact. Therefore, parents may seek out teachers for answers to questions
and for emotional support.

One of the first considerations is to inform parents of the
nature of the proceeding itself. They need to know who will be
participating, where the meeting will be held, how long it will
last. The teacher can be helpful in explaining the terminology
that will be used. The teacher can request all reports of testing
be sent to the parent ahead of time. Often a preconference with
the parents is advised to answer any questions and explain the
types of questions that will be asked. At this time information
can be solicited from the parents with respect to the child's
developmental history, school history, and attitudes from the
parents' perspective. This preconference meeting will help foster a positive rapport between the family and the school and set
a cooperative tone for the IEP itself.

At the IEP meeting, assessments will be analyzed and interpreted. Then, a specific plan will be developed for the forthcoming
year. The parents will need to have explained how the plan will
be specifically implemented. They will want to know what is
expected of them. They will want to know the details of schedul-
ing, times, locations, and transportation, if appropriate. They will
want to know what instructional approaches and behavioral strategies will be used. The parents will continue to need the support
of the teacher who can help them maintain a positive outlook. The
teacher can emphasize the strengths of the student and point out
where to look for progress in the future.

Teachers Are Not Counselors

Although in this chapter, and throughout this book, we have
spoken to you about those situations in which you will be
functioning like a counselor, you have not had the specialized
training (usually the equivalent of two years of full-time study—a
48-hour masters degree) to be counselors. The skills we have
presented and the knowledge base we have introduced are only

a rudimentary background to help you prepare better for the multiple roles you will play in your profession.

Unfortunately, in spite of your best intentions to address all of the needs of your students—psychological as well as academic—you will just not have the time to do the complete job that you would prefer. Your hands will be more than full keeping up with your instructional responsibilities and the support activities that go along with them. Nevertheless, we have shown you a number of ways to integrate counseling methods and skills into your interpersonal style and classroom environment.

What would you like your students to say about you 10 years from now? How would you most like to be remembered by all the kids that you will come into contact with throughout your career? It would be nice if they remembered that you taught them some important things about life, the world, and themselves. But even more fulfilling—imagine that they'll say you really cared about them. You were there for them, really there. They will remember that you were a great listener, someone whom they could trust. You were someone who saw them as individuals. You did not judge them nor did you criticize them (even though you were critical of their self-defeating behavior). They will remember that to you, teaching was not just a job. It was not just something that you did. A teacher is who you were. A teacher is who you are.

Suggested Activities

1. Answer the following questions in a journal or small group discussion: Who were the teachers who inspired you the most in your life? What were they like, and what did they do that made the most difference to you?
2. How would *you* most like to be remembered as a teacher? If a group of your former students were to meet 20 years from now and talk about you, what would you like them to say?
3. Interview a school counselor, a school psychologist, a university professor, and an administrator to find out how they perceive their roles as consultants to teachers.

4. Make a list of the situations, problems, and concerns that you feel least prepared to deal with. Start building a resource file of experts in the community with whom you could consult about those situations. Compile a list of resources and support groups that are also available.

5. Based on the topics we have covered in this book, and what you have learned, make a commitment to follow through on three resolutions that you believe are important to your role as a teacher. Share them in a group or write them down.

Suggested Readings

Dougherty, A. M. (1990). *Consultation: Practice and perspectives.* Pacific Grove, CA: Brooks/Cole.

MacMillian, C. (1988, September). Suggestions of classroom teachers about designing the I.E.P. *Exceptional Parent*, pp. 90-92.

Phillips-Jones, L. (1982). *Mentors and proteges.* New York: Arbor House.

Rosenfield, S. A. (1987). *Instructional consultation.* Hillsdale, NJ: Lawrence Erlbaum.

Simpson, R.L. (1990). *Conferencing parents of exceptional children.* Austin, TX: Pro-Ed.